Songwriting

From Ideas to Royalties

About the Author

Joe Keene

Born: Clinton, Kentucky, attended grade and high school in New Madrid, Missouri and graduated in 1956. Now resides in Kennett, Missouri.

Began his career in the music business as a performer with his own band in October 1956. Recorded for: ARA, RENAY, KSS, and J*E*K International Records. Retired as a performer and recording artist May 9, 1987.

Owns four music publishing companies and three record labels. Built Kennett Sound Studios, Inc. in 1971. Served as president and chief engineer through December 31, 1997.

Songwriter, with over seventy songs recorded, including a song in a number one, million selling album by country music superstar Charley Pride.

Began writing novels in 1985. First book, *Baby Grand,* a horror story published by Zebra Books in August 1987, was co-written with longtime friend, William W. "Bill" Johnstone. Bill also worked with Joe in the music business, as a drummer, in 1958 and 1959.

Writes: horror, adventure, contemporary romance, and mainstream novels. Has been published in all print categories: fiction, nonfiction, magazines, newspapers, songs and poetry. Joe's most recent writing success was for the stage. His stageplay, *Mama's Front Porch* was produced in October 1996.

Conducts workshops on songwriting and book writing and is a featured speaker at a number of the nation's most popular writers conferences, including:

Golden Triangle Writers Guild, Beaumont, Texas
Mississippi Writers Association, Jackson, Mississippi
Heartland Writers Guild, Cape Girardeau, Missouri

Other Facts and Figures:

Military Service: Served in U.S. Army, October 1961 – October 1963, honorably discharged.

Radio: Ten years experience in broadcasting, with radio stations KMIS, Portageville, MO, KBOA, Kennett, MO, WKTA, McKenzie, TN, WFWL, Camden, TN, and with Armed Forces Radio during military service years. Twice honored by WSM radio in Nashville, Tennessee as Mr. D.J. USA.

Record Producer: Has produced hundreds of records for both aspiring recording artists and nationally known performers, including demo recordings for seven time Grammy award winner Sheryl Crow. In 1991, produced and engineered a twelve song album project for Stephen Ackles, one of Norway's most popular recording artists. The album was nominated for a Norwegian Grammy.

Songwriting

From Ideas to Royalties

by

Joe Keene

SKYWARD PUBLISHING, INC.

Dallas, Texas
www.skywardpublishing.com
skyward@sheltonbbs.com

Copyright ©2001 by Skyward Publishing, Inc.

Publisher: Skyward Publishing, Inc
             Dallas, Texas
             Marketing: 813 Michael
             Kennett, MO 63857
             Phone: 573-717-1040
             Fax: 413-702-5141
             E-Mail: skyward@sheltonbbs.com
             Website: www.skywardpublishing.com

Library of Congress Cataloging-in-Publication Data

Keene, Joe, 1938-
     Songwriting: from ideas to royalties / by Joe Keene.
          p.   cm.
     ISBN 1-881554-10-4
     1. Popular music--Writing and publishing. I. Title.

MT67.K44 2001
782.4216413--dc21

                                          00-054733

Printed in the United States of America

*Dedicated to the memory of my father, Harold Keene,
my mother, Lucille Keene, my brother, Eddie Keene,
and to my sister, Virginia Keene Brawley.*

Table of Contents

Introduction		13
1	Ideas	19
2	Titles	29
3	Synopsis	37
4	Opening Lines	43
5	The Hook	47
6	Form or Structure	53
7	Rhythm, Rhyme, and Tempo	57
8	Melody and Chord Progressions	63
9	Imagery	67
10	From A to Z --Writing the Song	73
11	Judge and Jury--What's the Verdict?	79
12	Collaboration	95
13	Find Your Audience	101
14	All Through--What Now?	107
15	Publishers--What Are They Looking For?	113
16	Contacts	119
17	Copyrights	125
18	Royalties	131
19	Bits & Pieces	139
20	Organizations	147
21	Credits and Permissions	151

Acknowledgements

Elvis made me do it.

In the late spring of 1956, after graduating from high school in New Madrid, Missouri, I spent three months in Indianapolis, Indiana, with my friend Buddy Bellon, his mother Evelyn, and his father Sid.

During June, July, and August of that long, hot summer, while searching for what I wanted to do with my life, I caught a severe case of "Elvisitis." In some circles, this malady is known as the rockin' pneumonia and the boogie woogie flu. Like many other young men in America, I was swept up in the swirl of rock 'n' roll and rockabilly music, the kind of music played and performed by Elvis Presley, Carl Perkins, Jerry Lee Lewis, and scores of other practitioners of the new carefree, don't -take-it-too-seriously musical art form.

After returning to New Madrid and purchasing my first guitar on October 15, 1956, I spent the next 30 years and 7 months having the time of my life, meeting and sharing the stage with some of the biggest names in the music business and countless others who labored on the lower rungs of the music business ladder.

To even begin to mention everyone who has touched my life, influenced me, or inspired me would take way too much time and mean little or nothing to most readers, and I would surely leave out someone very important. So, I will mention only a few and apologize to all others for the omission.

To Billie and Velma French, thanks for being my first loyal fans.

To Bill Johnstone, Narvel Felts, Tom Rasberry, Roland Janes, Steve Sharp, Dennis Nail, David Lemonds, Jamie Holmes, Gary Wilcoxson, Daryl Wilcoxson, Charles Isbell, and Terry Ray Bradley, thanks for being such loyal friends.

To Steve Wilkerson, thanks for growing up to be the great musician that I thought you would be.

To my brothers, Marvin and Johnie, who believed in what I was doing when others did not.

To Kay, thanks for giving me my wonderful sons, Scott and Kelly.

To Kelly and Larry, thanks for giving me two fantastic grandchildren, Jake and Jenna.

And last, but not least, thanks to Donna for everything else.

J.E.K.

Introduction

Given the choice, most writers would probably like to begin with the last link of the songwriting chain: the royalties. Unfortunately, it doesn't work that way. Songwriting, when it is pursued in a professional manner, is a business. And like any other business, a great deal of hard work must be done before any royalties can be harvested.

As it is with other endeavors where one-of-a-kind things are being created, songwriting instruction can only take you so far. When this point has been reached, after all the inspiration, motivation and instruction has been imparted, you have to take over and do the actual creating yourself.

Though this is not to imply that either is an art form, riding a bicycle or playing tennis can be used as examples. One can only experience the full effect of the activity in the actual participation of it.

This part of the songwriting process, the fact that so much of the craft cannot be taught, has always left me a bit frustrated. Past a certain point of instruction, a writer is always on his own. And being so is usually not the most comforting feeling in the world.

The seed of the idea for this book was planted in 1989 when the conference coordinator of the Golden Triangle Writer's Guild in Beaumont, Texas, invited me to conduct their first songwriting workshop.

The GTWG conference, a four-day affair held in mid-October each year, is one of the most popular writing conferences in the nation. It's also one of the best. The conference features workshops conducted by some of the most successful writers, editors, agents, and publishers in America. All categories of writing are represented: fiction, nonfiction, poetry and screenwriting. And, of course, with all this heavyweight talent as the draw, the conference attracts writers, aspiring and otherwise, from over half the states in the nation. (In a typical year, writers from at least twenty-six states are in attendance.)

The conference's reputation for excellence was well known to me, so I immediately accepted the invitation to add songwriting instruction to their list of workshops. Of course, I was asked if I had a title for my workshop. I didn't at the time, but I soon came up with one: the title of this book, *Songwriting: From Ideas to Royalties*.

Attaining success in any field of endeavor usually depends on a great number of things, way too many to single out any one element as the primary reason for success. Rather than merely touching on one part of the songwriting process, I felt that I should be prepared to discuss the business of songwriting from one end of the spectrum to the other; from conception to reward; from ideas to royalties.

I can't remember a time when I have not been interested in music. Like everyone else, I was first a fan.

I took my first step toward being a professional in October of 1956 when I purchased my first guitar. Within six months, I had formed my own band.

From that time to this, music has played a major role in my life, both personal and professional; so much so that it's difficult to determine where one ends and the other begins.

From a guitar-playing performer, I eventually broadened my musical interests by learning to play other instruments: the piano, electric bass, and drums. One step led to another: a recording career, then building my own recording studio, producing records, establishing publishing companies and record labels.

And through all this, I was writing songs, songs for my own recording needs and songs for others artists, some who enjoyed only nominal success but many others who were quite familiar with the top of the national record charts.

The writing of each song was a new experience. As it is with most writers who are serious about their work, I learned something new with each additional creation. But no matter how much I knew, or how much knowledge I attained, there was that much more to be learned. It seems to be a never-ending process.

And perhaps that's part of the attraction of the craft: Saying things the way you want them said, expressing the way you feel. Creating more and better songs and learning more each time the exercise is performed; feeling yourself grow, and realizing that each experience is taking you a step closer to being what you might be, or at least tapping another vein of your talent potential.

The urge to write is an itching of the soul. You have no choice but to scratch.

For those afflicted with this incurable malady, it is my hope that the thoughts contained within these pages will aid you in combating what ails you, not to cure you but to make your scratching more effective.

In preparing this book, many hours have been spent trying to think of as many specific things as possible about songwriting that might be included in this work. There are many things that I have found to be extremely beneficial in my own songwriting efforts. Hopefully, they will be of the same benefit to you. Perhaps in some small way they will aid you in becoming a better writer. Perhaps one day I will be fortunate enough to enjoy the fruits of your labor. If so, I will be well-paid and richly blessed.

Keep on scratching!

In the early days of Hollywood, a young man named Irving Thalberg left New York and went to California. He worked first for Carl Laemmle at Universal Pictures. Then, in 1923, he went to work for Louis B. Mayer at the Mayer Company.

In the spring of 1924, when Metro and Goldwyn joined forces, to eventually become Metro-Goldwyn-Mayer, more commonly known as M-G-M, Irving Thalberg was named the head of production. This young man, only 25 years old at the time, was responsible for producing and releasing a motion picture each and every week of the year.

Irving had been an office manager and a production assistant. He was now in charge of production, but he was not a producer. He was not a director, a cameraman, a set decorator, a costume designer, a lighting technician, and he was not a writer. He had no expertise in any one of the jobs necessary for the production of fine motion pictures. But Irving had something more, a rare and special gift. He could look at a piece of work and accurately judge whether it was right or wrong.

If there was something wrong, he could usually suggest the things that could be done to make it right. This was his greatest talent.

He admired and appreciated writers, but he had no more understanding of what writing was about than he did the other aspects of the movies.

Hollywood was teeming with famous writers during the glory days of the motion picture industry. Anita Loos, Dorothy Parker, F. Scott Fitzgerald, George S. Kaufman and many others worthy of being mentioned in company of this stature were in the city, all contributing something to the dream factory.

During a lull in a writer's meeting at M-G-M one day, Irving commented that he did not understand why everyone made such a big deal about writing.

"It's merely putting one word after another," he judged, adding a dismissive shrug of his shoulders to the brief statement.

After a moment of silence, one of the writers spoke. "No, Mister Thalberg. It's putting one 'right' word after another."

Those words were spoken more than half a century ago, but they're still true.

And that's what this book is all about — putting one "right" word after another.

```
: . . . . . . . . . . . . . . . . . . . . :
:                                         :
:          Chapter 1                      :
:                                         :
: . . . . . . . . . . . . . . . . . . . . :
```

Ideas

"It All Begins With A Song" is the motto of the Nashville Songwriter's Association.

That's a great motto, and the statement is true when speaking of the craft of songwriting as it relates to performing live or to the recording process. To perform or to record, an artist must have a song.

But here, we're concerned with something more: where did the song come from?

Songwriting usually begins with an idea. But many times it actually begins at an earlier point, when a young man wishes to express his feelings for his girlfriend more fully than with the three little words with which we're all familiar.

"I Love You" might properly express the young man's feelings, but the phrase has been used so indiscriminately over the years that the three words alone are no longer adequate for everyone.

Desiring to express his feelings more fully, and perhaps wishing to be more creative, the young man takes pen in hand and begins to write, committing to paper the words that might more appropriately express his feelings.

In the midst of this creation, perhaps he stumbles onto a rhyme. Prior to this, songwriting might have been the furthest thing from his mind. But at this moment, the young man tells himself: I'm going to write a song.

That's when the fun begins.

At one time or another, almost every man, woman and child will try to write a song. It might be a variation of an existing song, composed by substituting your own lyrics for those in a song you've heard, perhaps personalizing it to your needs or to suit your own situation.

But sooner or later something will happen to you and, inspired by the joy, the pain, or whatever emotion the occurrence evoked, you will make up your own lines, and probably your own melody.

If the experience were satisfying and the results enjoyable, you might begin to search for other things to write about, taking things more seriously, perhaps telling yourself that you want to be a real songwriter.

That's when the work begins.

A serious songwriter, a professional or one aspiring to be, thinks of little else but writing songs. He will be attuned to the world around him, to the things people say, the things they do, how they act and react, always alert for something to write about.

Writing is easy. Writing something unique and doing it well is a bit more difficult.

If you're in love with someone; wife or husband, boyfriend or girlfriend, sooner or later you will be inspired to tell them so, using more than three words and in some poetic form. It might be nothing more than a poem consisting of four lines.

Those with more talent, showing off their way with words, might go on to write eight, twelve or sixteen lines. Having done so, you might be inclined to consider yourself a songwriter. Maybe so. But of what expertise? Of what quality was your effort? You may have expressed your feelings perfectly, heartfelt and totally sincere. But your personal feelings do not necessarily mean that your effort is a good song.

The idea comes first. Expressing the idea comes second. But before doing the second, you need to pass judgment on the first.

- ♦ How good is your idea?

- ♦ Is it really different?

- ♦ Will it really make a good song?

- ♦ Can you write it and make it so?

In many ways, you have to approach songwriting the same way a carpenter builds a house. Before construction can begin, a carpenter has to have some idea of what he's going to build. He usually has a set of blueprints to work from.

The blueprints will include the floor plan. The floor plan will specify how big each room will be, where the walls and doors will be, and where the plumbing and electricity will be.

A carpenter can work from previously used blueprints, but the house he builds will not be original. For that, he needs blueprints never used before and a floor plan never used before.

To be original, that's what your song has to be, an

idea never before expressed in the manner you are now doing. With fresh blueprints and a new floor plan, the carpenter assembles materials and tools and begins his work.

For most songwriters, the materials will be paper and a pencil, and perhaps a rhyming dictionary and a thesaurus. Those with some musical ability might also use a piano or a guitar, devising a melody to fit your words.

The carpenter will begin by pouring a foundation.

A songwriter's foundation is his idea, possibly a title, one hinting of what the song will be about.

With the foundation in place, the carpenter will then begin constructing walls, using two by fours, two by sixes and two by eights, lumber similar to what he's used in every other structure he's ever built.

A songwriter will begin to erect his walls, too, using many of the same words that have been used in every other song ever written, but stringing them together in a new way, one fresh enough and catchy enough to grab someone's attention and make them want to hear what the next line will be.

The carpenter will use nails to hold everything together.

The songwriter will use nails, too, but there will be a difference. And that difference is the idea. That and the new way you string those same-old-everyday words together.

The carpenter will finish by putting the roof on.

The songwriter tops off his work by carefully going over every word and every line, evaluating, judging, changing and substituting, polishing everything, making sure that his idea is on the paper and not in his head. And making certain that he's chosen the right combination of words to best express his idea.

At this point, the process is much like squeezing juice from an orange. If your idea is good, you can't afford to waste it. Squeeze until every drop is on the paper. But be patient.

Write the song today. Look at it again tomorrow. Maybe you can squeeze another drop out of it. If not, then let it be. All you can do is all you can do.

Once you've done your best, when you're certain that you've exploited the idea to the fullest, put your name on it and go to something else.

Ideas: Where to Get Them

The first place to look for song ideas is your own life. The things you've done can be your own private storehouse of song ideas, a supply that no one else can touch. Only you know all the things that have happened to you, so your personal experiences are yours to use as you choose.

Your Feelings

Think of things you like and dislike, things that make you laugh and cry; all are potential subjects for songs.

Love has always been the most popular subject for songs and it probably always will be. So, if you're in love, take a good long look at your feelings, explore them, and think of a different way to express the way you feel.

It's very possible that you'll discover something that has not been said before. This discovery can move you to new areas that when explored can be the focus of songs you've never thought of before.

Your Imagination

In many ways, the things you might imagine can be even better than your true experiences. With your imagination, you're exploring what might have been in addition to what actually was.

Tell Someone Else's Story

Pay close attention when you're with your friends, relatives, and other acquaintances. Listen to what they say, as they tell of things they've done and how they feel about things. Their lives and experiences can be another rich source of song material.

Novelty Songs

Though they're not an everyday music business staple, a witty, well-written novelty song will always find a place in popular music. A recent good example is the Christmas-oriented song, "Grandma Got Run Over by A Reindeer." The first year the song was on the market, it enjoyed only minimal success. But in the years since its release, the song has grown in popularity, now garnering almost as much radio airplay each holiday season as the older, more traditional Christmas classics.

Unusual Characters or Situations

Songs about unusual characters or unusual situations will also be worthy of your time and consideration. As a songwriter, you must consider everyone and everything as a potential song source.

Previously Written Songs

If you're already a songwriter, another source of new material is your own songs. Examine your previously written songs. Perhaps hidden in one of the lines you'll find the foundation for another song.

Another Point of View

Another slant to take is to rewrite a man's song, telling it from a woman's point of view. Many answer songs have been written in this manner, sometimes by doing nothing more than changing the gender words: he and she, him and her.

But there are other variations that can be exploited as well. Men and women express themselves differently and their feelings about things will not be the same.

Try to imagine what the woman's viewpoint would be and use it for the basis of a new song. Women writers can do the same, telling the story from a man's point of view.

Positive or Negative?

There are songs about winning and there are songs about losing. There are those people who seem to gloat in misery, dwelling on the sad, dark side of life. But most people seem to enjoy hearing something about winning, songs told from a positive point of view.

Songs are short stories, and most people look forward to happy endings, where things turn out well in the end, as most people hope their lives will be. Write the song as you truly think it should be written, whether negative or positive, but before deciding your course, take a good look at both sides. Good ideas are precious and few. Don't overlook or reject other good possibilities.

Write Your Ideas Down

Perhaps it should have been said before now, but one of the first things a writer should do is write things down – always. Do not confuse memory with creativity. They're not the same.

A famous singer/songwriter once said that he never actually committed his songs to paper as he was creating them. He merely sang them, repeating each line over and over until he had reached the end of the song.

The next day, he would sing the song again. If he remembered all the words, he surmised that the song was good. If he didn't recall everything, it must have been bad.

This writer had enjoyed a great deal of success, so he obviously had been doing something right. But it's amazing that he handled his creations in such a careless manner.

Memory is one of God's greatest gifts. A good memory is one of our most valuable tools. But it is impossible to remember everything. Having this human frailty, and having to cope with it, man invented pencil and paper.

Write it down. The moment of creativity can be brief and fleeting. Preserve your thoughts by utilizing something more than your memory.

Compare your writing to a live performance. Perform live and your audience will be limited in size, no larger than the number of seats available in the auditorium in which you're performing. The performance is also gone after you're finished. Record it and you can share it with the ages.

Writing Creates Magic

A strange thing happens when you write. In the beginning, the more you write, the more you want to write. It's similar to being in love, especially for the first time. It's all you can think about.

After a while, the more you write, the less you write.

This happens when you've developed some expertise and the ability to judge and be objective about your work. You still like the process as much, but now you've become more discriminating, more particular, more demanding of yourself and the words you use to express your thoughts. Twelve or sixteen lines of words will no longer suffice. They must be lines filled with the right words, words expressing thoughts of excellence.

You will write less because of discarding the ideas that are unworthy of your time. But there is a plus side to this. What you do write will be much better. You might experience another curious thing, too. For most writers, finishing a song frees two emotions: Happiness and Sadness. Happiness from having created something new. Sadness that you can no longer work on it. But that's the price you pay for having the gift of creation.

Chapter 2

Titles

The title of your song is your brand name; it should be chosen with care. The more memorable the title, the more lasting the impression it will make when it is read and when it is heard.

Of course, the words behind the title, the lyrics of your song, will have to be strong enough to fulfill the idea the title promises. But many titles are weak and vague, promising little of interest and usually getting a like amount of attention.

Ideally, titles should express a complete thought or something close to it.

Two examples from my own work are: "Don't Start Something You Can't Finish" and "There's More Where That Came From." Both titles are complete thoughts, each giving a very good indication of what the song is about.

"Don't Start Something You Can't Finish" evokes visions of feelings being aroused by someone, a girl for instance. The admonition, coming from her boyfriend, is to avoid making promises she can't keep.

"There's More Where That Came From" is a man's promise to his partner that she should not be concerned that he will stop loving her or that his supply of affection will diminish or be exhausted.

The best song titles are those expressing complete thoughts. These titles are usually a bit easier for a listener to remember.

This is not to say that good songs have not been written that contained something less. "Stardust" is a great song. So is "Mood Indigo." There are many great songs that have no more than one, two, or three words in the title.

Songs with girls names as titles are plentiful, too. And there are many good ones. "Laura," "Marie," and even "Peggy Sue." But in these songs, the idea is hidden somewhere behind the title, an idea known only to the songwriter until being revealed as the lyrics of the songs are sung.

Professional songwriters or those who are serious about the craft, are always looking for words or phrases that might be used as song titles. Good titles might be found anywhere, so always be looking for them.

Start a file for song titles and store them away until you're ready to do the actual writing. Do the same thing with unusual lines or phrases or anything you find interesting. You're a writer so write them down.

Three fertile areas for titles are: what you read, what you hear, and what you can imagine.

What You Read

Magazines, newspapers, novels, or almost any-where words can be written, are good places to look for titles. Good songs have also been adapted from a phrase first found in an advertisement. Be a reader. You'll be rewarded in more ways than one.

What You Hear

Listening to what people say is also a rich store-house for song titles. Pearls of lyric wisdom have been known to fall from the unlikeliest of places, so always be attuned to what is being said, even when you think nothing of importance is being uttered. Become a good listener. Again, there's a good chance that you'll be richly rewarded for your patience.

What You Can Imagine

This area is usually the best. With things you read or hear, care should be taken to insure that you're not infringing on someone else's property. A great song title is not worth a plagiarism suit. Things born of your own imagination will usually be fresh and original, and free of any ties.

Note: Song titles cannot be copyrighted, but if you create a title from something you hear or read, it would be a good idea to make certain that the words, as you intend to use them, are not copyright protected. When in doubt, find out. Make a call and ask.

Choosing the Right Title

After a title has been chosen, take a look at it from all angles. You've already determined that it's a good title. But what if you've overlooked another possibility.

The best example of the benefits of this reevaluation process comes from my own experience. One of my

most successful songs is one recorded by Charley Pride.
The song was co-written with my good friend Charles
Isbell. In fact, the idea for the song came from Charles.
In addition to writing songs, we were both working in
radio at the time. Charles came in one morning, his face
all aglow. I soon learned why.

Charles had an idea for a new song. He told me the
title: "I've Just Found Another Reason For Leaving
You."

The title was interesting, but I immediately made a
suggestion: Change the word "leaving" to "loving."

This did two things: It changed the viewpoint from
negative to positive and instantly opened up many
things to say that could not be said from the opposite
point of view. Written from the positive viewpoint, the
song's message would have the potential to touch the
lives of more people.

Charles took only a second to pass his judgment on
the proposed change. He nodded his agreement, and
later, when we sat down to write the song, the words
came in a rush.

As it was being written, the song seemed to have a
Merle Haggard flavor to it. Later in the week, when the
song was recorded with a band, we still had Merle on
our minds. We had no working relationship with him
or his record label, but he was enjoying a great deal of
success and we were already thinking of how we might
present the song to him.

The day after the demo session, I again listened to
the tape. As I listened this time, another artist possibility came to mind. Something about the vocalist's
phrasing gave the song a Charley Pride touch.

At the time, we also had no working relationship
with Charley Pride, but I was familiar with the name of

the man who ran his office, a young southern gentle-
man named Tom Collins. I phoned, told Mr. Collins
why I was calling, and was instructed to forward the
tape to his attention.

To cut to the chase, everyone liked the song, Charley
Pride recorded it, RCA included it in the *Amazing Love*
album, and it sold lots and lots of records. Mr. and Mrs.
America — the fans — liked the song, as Charles Isbell and
I thought they would.

It feels good when you're right. I've often wondered
what fate the song might have enjoyed if it had been
written from the other point of view.

Perhaps that will be a future writing project, to
rewrite it in that manner. Who knows? We might end
up with another hit!

Word Association

Another valuable procedure to explore before
writing your song is that of word association. Within
your title there will be a dominant word, a word that
will suggest other words or phrases that are closely
related.

The song best demonstrating this comes from my
own work, a song entitled "Doctor Love." The
dominant word is doctor.

The words most closely related to doctor have been
capitalized in the lyrics, and you'll readily see how the
words fit with the dominate word.   Be creative and
play around with word associations until you develop
the right words for your song.

"DOCTOR LOVE"

I'm the love doctor, I can CURE YOUR ILLS,
I'm the love doctor, you don't need any PILLS,
Just sit right down and tell me all about YOUR
  CONDITION,
I'm sure the love doctor can FILL YOUR
  PRESCRIPTION,
I'm the love doctor, (doctor love,)
I'm the love doctor, (doctor love.)
I'm the love doctor, my MEDICINE is strong,
I'm the love doctor, and it won't take long,
I always MAKE MY ROUNDS no matter what the
  weather,
Just SHOW ME WHERE IT HURTS and I can MAKE
  YOU FEEL BETTER,
I'm the love doctor, (doctor love,)
I'm the love doctor, (doctor love.)

Chorus:
Doctor love is MAKING HOUSE CALLS all over town
  it's true,
I guarantee that you will FEEL BETTER when the
  doctor gets through, with you,

I'm the love doctor, I can EASE YOUR PAIN,
I'm the love doctor, make you FEEL BETTER again,
Anytime you NEED MY SERVICES you don't have to
  worry,
Just CALL DOCTOR LOVE, I'll be over in a hurry,
I'm the love doctor, (doctor love,)
I'm the love doctor, (doctor love.)

The song is rhythm and blues flavored, a medium
tempo song with a slightly arrogant flavor. But it's a fun
song and serves as a good example of word association.
   This exercise doesn't always render this many
associated words, but the process usually consumes

only a few minutes and it's always worth the time to explore the procedure. There might be instances where using this method will lead you to a richer vein of words than you first imagined.

Exploring for associated words will usually allow you to more fully express the idea behind your title.

One final thing that you should strive to do in regard to titles and ideas is to work to increase the size of your vocabulary. There is a widely held theory that to be successful in any endeavor one must have a mastery of your language. Possessing a broad vocabulary allows you to readily make choices that would otherwise be lost to you.

All the words you're ever going to need will be found in your dictionary. Become more familiar with it. It's the best friend a writer will ever have.

There are many formulas for success. All of them include a mastery of your language.

Chapter 3

Synopsis

What is your song about? Tell someone that you've written a song, and it's almost a sure thing that you'll be asked this question: What is your song about?

It's a simple question. The answer should be simple, too. Unfortunately, it hardly ever is. Telling someone your idea simply and concisely is one of the most difficult things about writing.

It takes practice to develop the knack of explaining what your song is about in only a few lines. Ideally, you should be able to cover the main points of your idea in one or two lines. If you can't do it within those boundaries, you probably need to give your song more thought.

Most popular songs consist of 12 to 16 lines. There will be the occasional song containing more, perhaps a song with a bridge, extending the length to 18 to 20 lines. Since the finished product will be no longer than that, a one or two line synopsis seems more than adequate space to explain your idea.

What is your song about? Use a book synopsis as an example. The book *Gone With The Wind* is lengthy. My hard cover copy contains 689 pages. But the central theme of the story can be told briefly, in one line.

Gone With The Wind is a story about a southern girl struggling to cope with her life and times during the Civil War.

For the countless millions who have read and enjoyed the Margaret Mitchell classic, this synopsis might seem entirely too brief and simple to adequately describe such a great piece of work. The story is much more complex than this, of course, but this one line, consisting of only 23 words, delivers the three basic elements that all stories must contain: setting, character, and conflict. In addition, it reveals the primary theme of the story.

That one line also contains four of the five W's of writing: Who, what, where, when.

♦ Who: a girl.

♦ What: her efforts to deal with her life and times.

♦ Where: the south.

♦ When: during the years of the Civil War.

Not bad for a one-line explanation. It might take some practice to become this familiar with your song, or be this proficient at synopsizing, but it's worth the time and effort to do so. Knowing the central theme of your story will assist you in keeping your thoughts focused on your goal as you write. Knowing exactly what your song is about will aid you in reaching the conclusion you desire. By clearly establishing and understanding your destination, you'll be better prepared to take your listener where you want him to go.

Imagine the main theme of your song as being the trunk of a tree. The tree might have many limbs, branches and leaves, but none would be possible without the trunk to hold on to. Your song might have many parts, but they're all attached to your main theme.

You have a good title, now determine how you're going to begin. Also think of how you're going to end. The process is comparable to planning a trip.

First, you determine where you're going. If you don't know where you're going, you won't be able to tell when you've arrived.

Next, you decide when you're going to depart. Only then do you begin to consider how you're going to get there. Do you take the interstate or do you prefer the scenic route?

The synopsis process is simply asking yourself: What is the point of this song? What is the goal? Sooner or later, the questions have to be answered, even if only in your mind.

The entire synopsis procedure is nothing more than an exercise to better acquaint yourself with the song you're planning to write. It's your song. The better you know it, the better off you'll be.

Again, it might be compared to determining the destination of your trip. You can go for a leisurely Sunday drive with no destination in mind or you can head straight for your goal.

Today, the attention span of most listeners is quite short. If you hope to gain and maintain their attention, take the interstate. The scenic route would probably be more leisurely and relaxing for you. If you're writing for yourself, take that route. But if you're writing for the space age market that today's music business has become, get in the fast lane and stay there.

As earlier stated, songs are short stories. The specifics of other forms of writing also apply to songwriting.

♦ Who: the narrator of the song.

♦ When: the time frame. When is the song taking place?

♦ Where: the setting of the song. Where are you?

♦ What: the action of the song. What's happening?

♦ Why: the reason for the events. Who or what caused it?

♦ How: the resolution. What are you going to do about it?

The beginning writer will probably not hesitate to accept the fact that all the above specifics will be found in most songs and that it's a good idea to ask them of yourself — and answer them — before beginning work on a song.

To an old pro, asking these questions might seem elementary and the answers understood. But they became so only after years of engaging in the writing process. The questions are always asked and answered. Experience allows them to be dealt with inwardly, acquired intuition doing most of the work.

What is your song about? Keep asking the question

until you can answer it as easily as telling someone your name. At that point, you'll be a step closer to being a pro.

And that's what this is all about!

Chapter 4

Opening Lines

Your idea is fresh, you've chosen a good title, and you've given an adequate amount of thought to where you're going with your idea. Now it's time to commit, time to determine how you're going to get there. To do that, you must take that first step toward your eventual goal.

Your opening line must be strong. It is the foundation on which the rest of your song will be built.

Those two lines are worth reading again, and they're worth remembering. This statement will be true, whether you're writing your first song or your hundredth song.

You have a story to tell, but before you can do so, you must get your listener's attention. The first thing said must reach out and grab the listener, demanding his attention, just as though you've grabbed him by the nape of the neck.

Think of the first line of your song as being a pretty girl or a handsome man. They're the ones who get the most attention when they enter a room. That first glance is crucial. The opening line of your song will be crucial, too. It will last only a moment, so prepare to take advantage of it. Begin by telling something important, something to make the listener want to hear what else you have to say.

There have been many memorable song openings. James Brown's scream to open his classic rhythm and blues recording of "I Got You" (I Feel Good) is a prime example. He gets your attention and then immediately makes his statement, telling you about his condition (I feel good) and why he has it (I got you.)

Another attention-getting opening is the Charlie Rich recording of "The Most Beautiful Girl In The World." The first word Charlie says is, "Hey!" You can't get much more explicit than that.

It won't always be possible to think of such dramatic openings, but don't let that deter you from trying to find something just as good.

Your opening line also establishes where your story begins, in regard to time and place. The choices of starting places are many. You might begin at the obvious place, today, and then theoretically work your way forward to some other day or time. You might begin by telling of an incident that happened yesterday or long ago, making the incident relevant by working your way forward to today, at last revealing to the listener what you thought would interest him and why.

You might begin at the end of a life, then regress to reveal things that transpired earlier. The Tom T. Hall composition "The Year that Clayton Delaney Died" is an excellent example. Mr. Delaney has already expired as the song begins. The narrator then tells you how he happened to know the man and why his passing is of interest.

Another Tom T. Hall song that nicely illustrates this starting place is "The Ballad of Forty Dollars." In this song, the deceased is being buried and the narrator is a little put out about it because the recently departed went without paying his debt, the forty dollars mentioned in the title.

There are many songs that seem to be suspended in time, mentioning only situations that need to be resolved. All of these starting places work nicely, so pick one that best fits your idea, then begin. Songs are not lengthy works, so changing your mind and picking a new starting place will not be extremely difficult if your first choice does not work out.

Open with a Thought-Provoking Statement

Once you've determined where your story will begin, get into it in an ear-catching way. Open with a thought-provoking statement or something that will give your listener a clue as to the song's setting, the characters or the conflict.

Bobbie Gentry's recording of her composition "Ode to Billie Joe" gets right to the business at hand, mentioning the date (when) and the setting (where) in the opening line. The first person narrator (who) and the activity (what) are mentioned in the second line.

Ms. Gentry goes on steadily, dispensing vital, relevant information with every succeeding line, leaving no blank spots or openings for her listener to escape. This is as it should be, opening with a good, solid line and then building on it, word after word and line after line until the tale has been told.

Some writers want to warm up before revealing anything of consequence. A song is not a lengthy novel; it's a short story. You have only 12 to 20 lines to tell your tale, so don't beat around the bush. Get to it and stay with it.

Think of your own expectations. When you hear a comedian, you expect him to say something funny as he opens his performance, something to get your attention. If he makes you laugh with his opening, there's a good chance that you'll stay with him throughout the performance.

This is what your song must do. Grab the listener's attention, then hold his attention until you've told your story.

If the first line of your song does not grab your listener, you're probably going to lose him to someone else. Work hard to keep that from happening.

Ideally, your finished song will be a seven-course dinner. Unfortunately, since time is of the essence and space is limited, all seven courses must be served rather quickly, almost at once. Make every course count.

Remember: Your opening line must be strong. It is the foundation on which the rest of your song will be built.

Chapter 5

The Hook

No one seems to know who first used the word "hook" to describe the element of a song that demands and holds a listener's attention, but it's a good one and we're grateful. Describing the desired key element in a composition has been made a bit easier by using this word. This key element, now popularly known as the "hook," was once called "the punch line." This, too, was an excellent defining phrase. It's still quite useful and will continue to be utilized when and where it's appropriate.

The term "the punch line" originated in comedy. It describes the final words of a joke. It's where the laughs will be found, providing the things that came earlier properly lead to that conclusion.

The Hook Is Remembered

The hook, as it is used here, might first be the title of your song. More often than not, this is the case and it's desirable.

The hook, or a variation of it, might also be found in the last line of your verses. It might also open your chorus.

And finally, the hook should close your chorus, making it the last thing your listener hears as the song ends.

The hook might be more formally defined as: title repetition or some other catchy element your listener can hold on to, something memorable enough to be recalled after the song ends.

Ideally, after hearing your song only one time, your listener will remember the key element of your song. If you've done your job well, that will be true. If asked, he should be able to tell you what the song is about. Even more ideally, he will go away repeating a phrase or a line from the song, or at least humming a portion of the melody.

A very good example of making a lasting impression, which is what the "hook" is supposed to do, is the Lynn Anderson recording of the Joe South composition "Rose Garden." After only one hearing, almost everyone remembers at least one line: "I beg your pardon, I never promised you a rose garden."

There are many other outstanding examples of exploiting a song's key element. But where hooks or punch lines are concerned, this is as good as it gets. If you can write something this memorable, even if it's no more than one line, as illustrated above, you'll be well on your way toward songwriting success.

By placing so much emphasis on the "hook" of your song, you might be inclined to think that the rest of your creation can be neglected. Not so. Every word and every line of your song is important, and each should be carefully chosen.

Think of your song as a chain, one that you're putting together. Care should be taken to insure that there are no weak links. Every word and line should be meaningful, each one adding something of value to the story you're telling.

If a word is weak, replace it with one that is strong. If a word is not quite right, replace it with one that is more appropriate. If a line is faulty or trite, rewrite it, substituting something more solid or original.

Like the links in a chain, every word of your song is important. But there are three vital areas where excellence is paramount if any lasting impression is to be made: Your title, your opening line, and your ending, as you deliver your hook/punch line.

There are instances where your title and punch line will be the same. As previously stated, this is desirable. Smoothly done, this gives you additional opportunities to set your hook, and to keep it set long after the song has ended.

But caution should be exercised in the number of times your hook is repeated. There's a fine line between being in the groove and in a rut. Creative repetition is one thing, boring is another. Know where the line is and take care not to cross it.

The heart of your song is the chorus.
Make it strong and healthy.

Most songs begin with a verse, opening by establishing a question that needs to be answered, a situation that needs to be addressed, or a problem that needs to be resolved. There are songs that open with a chorus, but the verse opening is generally more popular.

Think of a ladder as we explore what opening your song with a chorus is like. Choruses are more dynamic than verses. Opening your song with a chorus is comparable to beginning your climb up the ladder and somehow finding yourself already near the top. You don't have much farther you can go.

If you begin your song with a chorus, you'll have to end it, releasing all the climactic tension, then you'll have to drop back and begin to climb again when you add your verse.

Opening with a chorus works quite well with some songs. If this is the course you choose, make sure that your story is best served by this choice. A little experimenting, and an objective opinion, will quickly answer the question.

If your song opens with a verse, it is only prelude, serving to get you where you want to be so you can say what you really want to say. The point of your song will be found in your chorus. It's where you go for the knockout, giving your listener your hardest punch.

In the verse is where you plant the seeds of your idea. Your chorus is reaping the harvest.

Your verse asks questions. Your chorus answers them.

The verse, as it relates to the chorus, and the part it plays in relation to the complete song, might also be considered sexual foreplay. It's desirable and enjoyable. It adds richness and meaning to a relationship. But complete fulfillment will be achieved only in the joining of two bodies.

Complete fulfillment, as it pertains to your song, will be attained only when the chorus is reached. The verse allows you to get to the chorus, where you wanted to be in the first place.

Finally, further elaborating on the statement that the chorus is the heart of your song, the first verse of your song can be considered the arms. The second verse can be considered the legs. Arms and legs are extremely important, but, if necessary, one can function without them. Without the heart, life is over.

Without a strong, healthy chorus, you have no song.

Chapter 6

Form or Structure

What comes first? What comes next? What comes after that? Simply put, this chain of events is what songwriting form is all about.

There are no wrong notes in music. Any note played individually is perfect. But when other notes are added, and when they're played together as a chord, the additional notes should complement the root note, blending into a sound that is pleasing to the ear.

This same care should be exercised as you begin to link the various sections of your song together. These sections are:

◆   Introduction
◆   Verse
◆   Chorus
◆   Bridge

These are the basic song parts most commonly used in today's popular music. There are others, but these are the workhorses used most often.

The various sections can be joined together in any way you choose, so, in essence, the same thing that was said about notes can apply here. When it comes to writing, the only rule is that there are no rules.

There are procedures, however, and patterns — ones that have been employed over a long period of time — procedures and patterns that have come to be regarded as something of the standard way of doing things. The forms most often used in popular music are somewhat predictable, but they're comfortable and satisfying, and they've come to be accepted because of that.

In England, in the days of the wandering minstrel man, folk ballads consisted of verses. Within the lines of each verse, questions would be asked and answered, or a part of a story would be told. The next section, another verse, would be the same in form and would be sung using the same melody as the first. Only the lyric content would make it different from the preceding verse. These ballads were popular and entertaining, but they contained no dynamic choruses as might be found in the music of today.

As time passed and as the songs of one land reached another, other ways of doing things were introduced and, in time, became accepted. As more time went by, other musical forms came into being, all eventually finding their places in popularity.

In a loose way, a song might be compared to a jigsaw puzzle. The individual parts of both song and puzzle must be joined together before the big picture can be seen. But the comparison ends there. There is but one way that a jigsaw puzzle will fit together. With songs, there are many. Songs are more flexible, allowing the creator of the words and music to exercise even more creativity in choosing the way the verses, choruses, and bridges are strung together.

Form can be further illustrated by thinking of the nine innings of a baseball game. The first inning is played, then the second, and so on, until the end of the game is reached. There are contributing factors that might cause the game to be played in less than the usual nine innings or more than nine innings. Rain might cause the game to be shorter; a tied score might require extra innings to be played to establish a clear winner. Other than these instances, the form will never change. Inning one will always come first. Whatever transpires within the space of each inning will be the only variance.

Once again, however, a song enjoys the flexibility of its creator choosing the exact sequence of its verses and choruses.

The Parts of a Song

The Introduction

An introduction usually involves the instrumentation that you're utilizing to accompany your song. Songs beginning with vocals have always been rare. They remain so today. Though it might be brief, perhaps only a few seconds long, most popular songs begin with a musical introduction. The importance of strong, distinctive introductions can be compared to the importance of opening lines; they must be strong and catchy. They must grab your attention.

The Verse

As previously stated, most songs begin with a verse. As a songwriter, this is where you first begin to reveal what you have to say. Say something meaningful in the first line, and there's a good chance that your listener will stay to hear what you have to say in the succeeding lines. If he finds the verse interesting, you'll have a chance to lead him to the next part of the form.

The Chorus

If your listener is still around when the chorus is reached, he should find something of value, something of greater interest than he's enjoyed to this point. The chorus is the payoff you've been promising: The prize in the Cracker Jack box, if you prefer.

In chapter two, we talked about a song entitled "Don't Start Something You Can't Finish." The statement that title makes could be applied here. In the verse, you made a deal with your listener: A promise of things to come. In the chorus is where you'll be expected to pay off, to keep that promise, to justify the time he's invested in your song.

The Bridge

The bridge of your song is unique, in that it will not utilize the same chord progression as the verse or the chorus. The bridge, as it is commonly used today, is usually a short section after a second chorus. The bridge gives you the opportunity to add something more to your story, and to do it in a more distinctive way than you've done in either your verse or chorus. Many bridges employ a key modulation. If the main part of your song is written in a major key, another option is to begin your bridge by dramatically dropping into a minor key, the contrast further enhancing your song.

In all fields of popular music, gospel, blues, country, rock and roll, jazz, or whatever, certain forms for the linking of verse and choruses have come to be widely accepted.

One of the most popular forms is: Verse, chorus, verse, chorus. This form can be illustrated as follows:

- ◆ A - verse
- ◆ B - chorus
- ◆ A - verse
- ◆ B - chorus

Another popular form is: verse, verse, chorus, verse, chorus.

- ◆ A - verse
- ◆ A - verse
- ◆ B - chorus
- ◆ A - verse
- ◆ B - chorus

Another form is:

- ◆ A - verse
- ◆ B - chorus
- ◆ A - verse
- ◆ B - chorus
- ◆ C - bridge
- ◆ B - chorus

You can write the greatest words in the world, the greatest verses and the greatest choruses, but if they are not presented in an acceptable manner or linked together pleasingly, in ways that listeners have come to expect and approve of, you'll be writing for yourself.

As a songwriter, strive to choose the perfect form for the story you're telling. Depending on what you have to say, and how much, one of the above forms will probably be right for your song. What the song needs to properly display it should be your primary concern. If it feels right to begin with a chorus, do so. If it doesn't feel right, don't do it. Make another choice.

If the next song you write utilizes the same form as the previous one, take a long hard look at it. Is the form really right, or are you being restricted by your musical ability? If the latter is the case, take steps to broaden your musical talent.

If you feel frustrated or restricted by the musical forms of today, there are many options open to you. Wait a while for changes to occur. They will. Today's music bears little resemblance to music of the past, the music of the wandering minstrel man for instance.

Another option is to become a musical leader. Work within the accepted musical forms of today, master them, then gradually make the changes that you desire. That's what leaders do. They initiate changes, molding and shaping things to their liking.

But keep this in mind: If you get too far ahead of your followers, they will lose sight of you. You'll soon be alone, singing to yourself, as you were in the beginning.

Chapter 7

Rhythm, Rhyme, and Tempo

Rhythm

♦ Rhythm: windshield wipers swiping back and forth.

♦ Rhythm: the ticking of the clock at your bedside.

♦ Rhythm: the rocking of a chair or a cradle.

Rhythm is also the clickety clack of a train going down a railroad track, its speed constant, the giant wheels hitting the small gaps where the shiny steel rails are joined together, and weaving a magic spell with its distinctive sound.

Rhythm is everywhere, in the everyday events of life and in your song. It will be present from the first day of your life until the last. And it will be present from the first word of your song to the last. Even during moments of silence, rhythm is there, resting as a certain number of beats go by.

As you write your song, as you sing each line, the words and the way you say them will begin to establish a rhythm, even if there is no musical instrument to accompany you. The second line will further define what the rhythm will be. By the time you've completed your fourth line, perhaps reaching the end of a verse, you'll be well on your way to knowing whether the rhythm is right or wrong.

Your words are closely linked to two other musical elements: melody and harmony, and more will be said about them in chapter eight. Here, we're concentrating on the words, the accented words, the words that you emphasize, the words that you stress to help make your point. Emphasis will help determine melody, and it will also play a part in determining rhythm.

Rhythm is present in slow, moody ballads, but it's more apparent in songs that are uptempo, medium or very fast. In fast songs, the words come at you in a rush. Quarter notes will play a far more prominent role than whole notes. And, as a result, the songwriter and listener will feel a much greater sense of rhythm.

One is not right and the other wrong. They are merely different, one more noticeable than the other.

Rhymes

One of the most satisfying things in the world is a perfect rhyme.

> Mary had a little lamb,
> Its fleece was white as snow,
> And everywhere that Mary went
> The lamb was sure to go.

When it's right, it's right. The same is true in poetry, nursery rhymes, or songs. The rhyming lines in this nursery classic are the second and fourth ones, the last word on each line: snow and go. The writer might have used a two-syllable word in the fourth line, follow, for instance. The meaning would have been the same, but the feeling would have been wrong.

Where rhymes are concerned, perfection should always be your goal.

Achieving perfect rhymes remains one of the most difficult tasks a writer must face. To say exactly what you want to say and match it with a perfect rhyme every couple of lines is a goal not easy to reach. There are times when you'll have to settle for less than perfect rhymes, but never accept something less until all options have been explored.

One way to explore is to use all the available writing aids: dictionary, rhyming dictionary, and thesaurus. Many great songs have been written without these things being used. To those writers already possessing extensive vocabularies, these aids might be considered excess baggage, a nuisance or a bother. But if your vocabulary is limited, you can benefit by doing two things: Strive to increase it, and use all the help you can get. A carpenter would not hesitate to use a powered nail gun if the need was warranted. No one cares how you wrote the song, only that you did. Use all the tools available.

Tempo

The theme of your song, the subject matter you're covering, will play a big part in determining tempo as well. Serious songs, songs concerning death for example, will never be uptempo. On the other hand, comedy songs are almost always uptempo. There have been exceptions, but they're rare.

Imagine a song like "I Left My Heart in San Francisco" being performed at a fast tempo. It can be done. But the song is much more effective and dramatic when it's performed as it was written, as a ballad.

In the late fifties, many rock and roll artists enjoyed much success reviving old standards. Songs that previously had been recorded as ballads were re-recorded, but as uptempo rockers. Carl Mann's rendering of "Mona Lisa" is a good example. Conway Twitty also had a version of this song. Both renditions worked quite well and both enjoyed a great amount of success. But the classic treatment of the song remains the one by Nat "King" Cole, performed as a lushly accompanied ballad.

The lyric content of your song, the number of words in each line, will help dictate the rhythm. The subject matter will help determine the tempo. Allowed to settle, to be performed naturally, and comfortably, your song will establish its own pace.

Whether your song is fast or slow,
A perfect rhyme is the way to go.

Chapter 8

Melody and Chord Progressions

As stated in chapter seven, rhythm, rhyme and tempo are so closely related that it's difficult to discuss one without including one or more of the others.

Even when no musical instrument is being used as accompaniment, spoken words or words being sung will have all these elements. Melody and chord progression are the other close members of this family, and it's time to consider these things and take a look at how they affect your written words.

Except for the fact that harmony plays such an important role in most songs, words and music might be considered as husband and wife. They're a team, a happy one if they're right for each other.

This is what you're looking for.

The lyrics you've written are perfect. Your idea is fresh, your title is clever and descriptive, teasingly hinting of what is to come, your opening line is an ear-catcher, and your punch line is a killer.

Ideally, your melody has already been playing a

significant part in the creation of your lyrics. It's almost impossible to write 12 or 16 lines and to finish them without some indication of how the words will be sung.

But now, it's time to be sure. Close is not good enough. Perfect words deserve a perfect melody. Perfect, in this sense, is the melody that allows your song to be sung to reach its full potential.

The words of a song will make demands, to some degree dictating the direction they will take, telling you where they want the melody to go. That's why a much greater emphasis has been placed on the choice of words than on the choice of melody.

This emphasis is not to be construed as judging the melody to be of less importance than the lyrics; nothing could be further from the truth. But in the mainstream of popular music today, instrumental songs are in the minority. It is for this fact, and this fact alone, that the choice was made to concentrate more on the choice of words than on the choice of music.

To a great extent, a song will tell you where it wants to go. Most professional songwriters have found that this is true. There are words in your song that you want to emphasize, key words that will help you make your point. Inflection is used to do this. And as this is done, your melody takes shape, some words bending, others curving, up and down, some quickly, others more gradual.

If you're in the key of F, don't expect to hear the song yell, "Bd!" It won't happen. It also won't say C7, Dm, Gm, Am or any of the other chords that are closely related to F that might conceivably be used. But if you're listening, paying close attention to the direction your melody is taking, the perfect chord will eventually become clear.

Again, strive to see that your melodies are not being bound to your limited musical abilities. Many great songs employ only 3 or 4 chords. But these chords were probably chosen because they were right and were all the song needed rather than because of any limitations of the writer.

Increasing your vocabulary will allow you to write better lyrically. If you're creating your own melodies and choosing your own chord progressions, work to increase the musical choices available to you as well.

The more you know, the more you grow.
The more you learn, the more you earn.

The chord progression will be chosen to allow the melody to go where it should go. When it's right, the melody and the lyrics will be as one, blending together in a seamless, natural way.

Think of Fred Astaire and Ginger Rogers, the famous ballroom dancing team of stage and screen. They were separate people, but on the dance floor, they were as one, swinging and swaying, one move smoothly leading to the next, as though no other choice was possible.

Strive to make your song sound as natural and comfortable as an old favorite.

I've had writers come to me, asking if I would listen to a song they'd written, not to consider it for one of the recording artists I might have been producing, but to give an opinion as to whether they were infringing on someone else's melody.

In most cases, as far as my memory, experience, and musical knowledge would allow me to judge, I would find the melody to be original.

The writer was afraid he was infringing on another's work because the marriage of words and music was so perfect and natural that he couldn't believe that it was original.

In a way, this is a happy predicament to be in. No one can ever know all the melodies that are written, so these situations will continue to arise. But the cause for the concern, this perfect wedding of words and music, should always be your goal.

Everyone hopes to find that perfect someone. Every lyricist hopes for the perfect melody. Sometimes the two get together. And when they do, it's magic!

> ```
> :............................:
> :                            :
> :        Chapter 9           :
> :                            :
> :............................:
> ```

Imagery

What Do Your Ears See?

The answer to this question is what imagery is all about: creating pictures with our words; painting them, as the process has been described. To achieve this, vivid words are used — right, intense, or clear, as vivid is defined in the dictionary. A few synonyms are: dramatic, pictorial, or colorful. All are desirable and all assist in understanding what imagery is all about, as it pertains to songwriting and recorded music.

If you can make your listener aware of all the W's of writing: who, what, where, when, why, and the all important H — how, you've achieved the ultimate in vivid imagery. And vivid images are those that will be remembered the longest.

Nouns – Name of a person, place or thing.

Songs are stories, and stories are about people. You could write a song about Alcatraz, the former federal prison located in the bay between San Francisco and Oakland, California. But you can go only so far until you have to tell about people, in this case the notorious prisoners who once spent their days and nights behind the bars of that famous institution.

You might also write about things, as Carl Perkins did in his classic 1956 rockabilly smash "Blue Suede Shoes." Granted, those famous shoes left an indelible image, but the heart of the story concerned the young man wearing them, and his fear that someone was going to step on them.

In choosing the nouns of your song; the people, places and things, look for the unusual to write about. The unusual leaves an image.

Verbs - A word expressing action, existence, or occurrence.

The strength of any writing will be found in verbs; the action words. This is true whether you're writing fact or fiction, lengthy novels, short stories, magazine articles, or songs. The stronger the verbs, the more memorable the writing. But you must exercise care that the verbs you choose are appropriate for the story you're telling.

You might say, "He walked across the street." Your character is now on the other side of the road, but the verb that got him there has no particular zip or zing to it. He was transported in a manner that has no memorable style. He might have strolled, strutted, staggered, swaggered, or any number of other things, possibly even meandered, if that verb best suited your intention. Always consider other alternatives and explore other possibilities before coming to a final decision. If "walked" is still the best choice, go with it.

Choose your verbs with care. Make certain that they work for you, that they are assisting in creating the impression you want to make, and that they will leave the image you desire. As with all the other things concerning your creation, what's right for your song should always be the determining factor.

Adverbs – A Word which qualifies or limits a verb, or a word used to modify a verb, adjective, or another adverb, by expressing time, place, manner, degree, etc.

In writing, nouns and verbs might be considered the meat and potatoes of the craft. Adverbs and adjectives might be considered the seasoning; the salt and pepper so important in making things more tasty.

In songwriting, adverbs are almost nonexistent. Look at the words of your favorite song or any song for that matter. Find the words that modify or qualify the action words. Finding an adverb in most songs might be compared to trying to find an honest politician. It's not impossible, but it will take some effort.

Adjectives - A word used to limit or qualify a noun or other substantive.

Adjectives are used in songs a bit more often than adverbs, but they're still used sparingly. This is true for two reasons:

♦ There's simply not enough time for them in the framework of today's popular song.

♦ The need for them is small.

But by carefully using adjectives, employing them

if and when it's appropriate, you can paint the most memorable of pictures.

In the words of the song below, a beautiful Christmas ballad, the imagery portrayed by the lyrics is strong and vivid, but the adjectives and adverbs are few.

"Christmas Is Everywhere"

First verse:
FALLING snow, mistletoe,
and presents 'round the tree,
the sound of laughter in the air,
it's SWEET music to me.

Second verse:
SLEIGH bells ringing, a choir singing,
not a worry, not a care,
the world's AGLOW with love tonight,
Christmas is everywhere.

Chorus:
And in our town, a CHAPEL bell
is ringing LOUD and CLEAR,
reminding us it won't be long
till Santa will be here,

Third verse:
Wherever you may be tonight
remember to say a prayer
for peace on earth, goodwill to men,
and MERRY Christmas everywhere.

The dominant qualifying or modifying words in this song have been capitalized. For the sake of this comparison, articles (a, an, the) and possessive adjectives (our) have been ignored. Out of the total of 85 words in this composition, only 8 are adverbs or adjectives, yet the imagery is very good. It's the night before Christmas, there's snow on the ground, and there's hope that everything will be all right.

Use everything at your disposal; nouns, verbs, adverbs and adjectives, in the creation of your song. The bottom line is always the same: do what is right for the song. Do that, and you can't go wrong.

Chapter 10

From A to Z—Writing the Song

Even if you've never written a song before, it is my hope that by picking and choosing the main ingredients from the preceding chapters, by understanding them and by remembering them, that you will now have some idea of what the creation of a good song is all about.

I won't say a "hit" song. The factors that make a song a hit are usually determined by things well outside the realm of creation, and usually by things far outside the range of the songwriter's control. Even if your song is great, it can still remain obscure and unknown, unheard by anyone other than yourself or the members of your family.

There is a popular horse racing reminder that says: There's only one way to win, but there are a million ways to lose.

Songwriting success is normally not this cut and dried. In horse racing, and in the music business, there are many degrees of achievement. It's true that there's only one first place purse in racing. But at most tracks in America, second, third, fourth and fifth place finishers are not without some compensation for their efforts. It's also true, however, that most people only remember who was first across the finish line. Finishing anywhere but first in the Kentucky Derby is a shaky platform on which to build your racing career.

In this regard, horse racing and songwriting are quite similar. A song that has reached the number one position on the charts receives much more respect than number two. The same is true in other fields of activity where the order of finish is kept. We remember and reward those who won the Academy Award, not those who were nominated.

We've previously used a ladder as a symbolic way to measure success and to do so again seems appropriate. Like your quest for perfection in your work, your aim should always be to reach the top rung of the ladder; to be number one. To hit high, you have to aim high. To win big, you have to think big. But first, you have to create a product that deserves to be considered for success in the big-time.

There are still many more links in the songwriting chain that have to be put into place, and they will be. But at this stage we're still more concerned with the creation of your song than the myriad of things that might happen to it before it reaches its final destination.

From Opening Line to Punch Line

You have a good title. You've chosen all the words and phrases that might be associated with your title. You've written a synopsis that is crystal clear, and you have a thorough understanding of the story you want to tell. Based on the thought behind your title, you should also have some idea whether the song is going to be a ballad or an up tempo song.

Where Do You Go from Here?

This is where the work begins. The first line must be chosen. Choose it with care. Remember, it is the foundation on which the remainder of your song will be built. Your title should contain some indication of setting, characters or conflict. If it's the setting, visualize this setting, who's there, and concentrate on the point you hope to finally make with your song.

As you've probably already discovered, this is not only where the work begins, it's also at this point that you're on your own. You know the form; the content is up to you.

The content of your song depends on the depth of your vocabulary, on your knowledge of the subject you've chosen to write about, and on your ability to clearly and emphatically express yourself.

But even though you're on your own, there are still definite, helpful factors to guide you in the choices you make.

♦ Clarity: Choose words and lines that clearly state your thoughts.

♦ Emphasis: Choose words with strength and color, words that will allow you to make your point.

♦ Style: String your words together to form sentences that will allow you to tell a story as it has never before been told.

Clarity, Emphasis, and Style. These three words will serve as guidelines in making the choice of all your other words.

Once your opening line is in place, tell your story as you want it to be told, adding to your opening line, and working your way toward your punch line, ideally, the title of your song or a variation of it.

By now, you know that every word in a song is important, just as all four tires on a car are necessary for any significant forward progress to be made. It's a timeworn cliche, but "close" counts only in horseshoes and hand grenades. Strive for the perfect word to express your thoughts.

As you're writing a line, if the proper word fails to emerge, leave a blank space or put in the first thing you think of. Defective words can be replaced with proper ones during the rewriting phase.

Songwriting requires concentration. And concentration is keeping your eyes on your goal and considering all the possibilities of how you're going to reach it. As with most things, it requires little more than honest effort; asking yourself for your best and settling for nothing less.

On Second Thought: Rewriting, Revising, Polishing

There are those who consider writing to be the fun part of the creative process and rewriting to be the work part. In time, I'm certain that you will make up your own mind whether this judgment is true or false. Both stages of the creative process are time consuming. Whether it's work or not depends on the enjoyment you derive from the effort.

Once you've told your story, or when you've filled in all the lines that you've deemed necessary to do so, the rewriting process gives you the opportunity to go back and reevaluate everything.

Of course, some rewriting, revising and polishing begins even as you put the first words on the paper. For this reason, it's a good idea for songwriters to use pencils rather than ballpoints or ink pens. It's also important to have a big eraser. The first words you choose are hardly ever your final choice. If you're being objective about your work, almost every time you read or sing a line, other choices will occur to you. If a new word occurs to you, and you think it might be better, jot it down, immediately. Remember, do not confuse memory with creativity.

Rewriting can be a time of agony. The choices are many and the more choices you have, the more difficult the decision making process can be. But sooner or later, you have to make up your mind, choose one word over another, put it on the paper and go on.

When you've reached this point, when you've actually written a complete song, you're way ahead of most people. Fifty percent of those who think about doing something will talk themselves out of it, whether it's writing a song or digging a ditch.

If you have the courage to continue, you have a good chance of succeeding. With every additional step you take, there's someone who's giving up. Another step, less competition. Stay with anything long enough and you'll leave most of your competition behind.

Ask a thousand people what success is and you'll get a thousand different answers. Success depends on how you define your particular goal, and only you can do it.

But there are a few traits that you will find present in everyone who has ever been successful, no matter what the activity:

- Preparation, patience, and persistence
- Especially persistence
- Preparation will get you started
- Patience will keep you going
- But it's persistence that opens the door

Persistence

"Nothing in the world can take the place of persistence. Talent will not; nothing is more common than unsuccessful men with talent. Genius will not; unrewarded genius is almost a proverb. Education alone will not; the world is full of educated derelicts. Persistence and determination alone are omnipotent." –Calvin Coolidge

....
Chapter 11
....

Judge and Jury—What's the Verdict?

You've finished your song. You think it's good. You have 16 lines, your rhymes are almost perfect, your chorus is powerful, your punch line is memorable, and a bit of the melody keeps running through your mind.

It's a good song. You know it is. Maybe even a great song. But something inside, something way down deep in your soul keeps nagging at you. You've overlooked something. The song appears to be perfect, but you're certain that there's something wrong with it.

♦ Who do you trust?

♦ Who do you listen to?

A songwriter with years of experience will probably no longer have these doubts or ask these questions. He will be his harshest critic, his best critic. He's earned the right. He's studied his market. He knows what's been done before and he's aware of what's being done today. He knows what works and what doesn't work. He's a pro and his goal is to do his best. He's even looked ahead, envisioning what the songs of tomorrow will be like.

If he's successful, he's also learned to be brutally honest in his opinion. If there are flaws in his song, he'll usually find them, and they will be eliminated long before the song is out of his hands.

Many writers, especially beginning ones, suffer from an incurable malady: failing in love with the first words they put on the paper. In songwriting, this is a weakness; one to be overcome as quickly as possible. If you're right the first time, fine. But if you're not, be willing to admit it and sensible enough to change. There are times when warm personal preferences have to give way to cold objectivity.

It's been said before, but it bears repeating: do what's right for the song. If you don't know what's right, get help. Find someone you trust, someone whose opinion you value, and someone who will tell you the truth.

The first place a fledgling writer usually looks for judgment is his wife, the members of his family, or his best friends. Unless they're experienced in the music industry, they can't be trusted. Too often, wives, family members and friends will tell you what they think you want to hear. You're too close to them and they don't want to hurt your feelings.

You learn from losing, not winning.

If they tell you your song is good, and you accept their word, you'll be satisfied with your efforts and you'll quit trying to grow and improve.

Maybe your song is good, even great. But don't rely on family members or friends to make the judgment. If you're sick, you go to a doctor. If you need legal advice, you go to an attorney.

If you have doubts about the excellence of your song, seek the opinion of someone in the music industry or, more ideally, an experienced songwriter or music publisher. If they think the song is good, they'll usually tell you why. If they think it isn't, if time permits, they'll also tell you why. If you're lucky, and if your song has any redeeming value, they may even tell you what might be done to improve it.

To simplify your songwriting efforts, your long-term goal should be to not only develop your skills as a songwriter but to be able to impartially judge your work as well. How can this be done?

In Detroit, and in other car manufacturing capitals of the world, an automobile company will buy a car made by their competition. An engineering team will take the car into a clean room and completely disassemble it. During disassembly, notes will be taken about how things were put together and each part will be carefully inspected. This procedure is helpful in determining what the competition is doing and how they're doing it, but it's time consuming and it's costly.

In all fields of writing: fiction, nonfiction, newspapers, magazines, poetry, or songwriting, checking out the competition is not nearly this complicated. Nor is it as costly. Soft cover books are from $10 to $19 each and hardcovers might run $20 or more. But this is considerably less expensive than a car, where the price range can be anywhere between $10,000 and $150,000.

In writing, where form and content is concerned, there are no secrets. (How the decisions were made is the only thing missing.) Open the pages of any book and you can see what the writer did and how he did it.

Open the pages of a song book or a piece of sheet music.
Read the words, then sing them. Check out the rhythm,
the rhyme, and the melody.
It's all there for your inspection.

♦ How does your song compare to theirs?

♦ Do you still have work to do?

If you have no expertise in judging the excellence of
songs, begin to develop a skill for doing so by
comparing your work with the work of others, those
who are successful in their field. But compare your
work to the best, not the worst.

You can learn from the best.
The worst can learn from you.

Buford Peek Memorial Show
Nov. 23, 1959

Jack Adkins, Bill Johnstone, and Joe Keene at piano

*What a thrill—playing two shows with Fats Domino
in April, 1964, after the release
of my first record.*

Joe Keene - Buford Pusser - Narvel Felts
September 2, 1973

Buford Pusser - Joe Keene
September 2, 1973

Ralph Emery
WSM Radio Studios - 1967

Billy   Walker-Bob   Luman-
Tex   Ritter-   Joe   Keene--Bobby   Lewis
"Being   around   these   big   stars   sure   is
exciting!"

Joe Keene - Archie Campbell
Nashville - 1967

Jimmy Pierce - Winnie Breast - Joe Keene
and the world-famous Jordanaires

Narvel Felts - Joe Keene - Jerry Foster

Joe Keene

Joe Keene

··························
:   :
:   Chapter 12   :
:   :
··························

Collaboration

Why Do It?

If you're proficient in all facets of songwriting: words, melody, harmony, rhythm and rhyme, writing with someone, or having someone write with you, is probably out of the question. There are those writers who know what they want to say, how they want to say it, and since they're good at it, their names appear alone as the composer of their songs.

Hank Williams, one of the most famous names in country music, needed little or no help composing his songs. It's true that Fred Rose, co-founder of Acuff-Rose Publications, and co-owner during the William's years, made periodic contributions to Hank's compositions. But he did so more in the context of performing his role as Hank's publisher than as his co-writer. Hank Williams' straightforward blend of words and music was natural and simple and one would be hard pressed to improve on his creations.

There are many other noteworthy writers who composed alone or are doing so at the present time.

Otis Blackwell, the writer of many Elvis Presley hits, — "Don't Be Cruel" and "All Shook Up" are two of the most famous — did much of his writing alone. And though he was quite capable of creating both words and music, he also worked with co-writers from time to time, one of whom was Jack Hammer. Otis and Jack wrote many fine rock and roll songs together. The classic Jerry Lee Lewis hit, "Great Balls Of Fire" is but one.

Mac Davis, the writer of "In The Ghetto," "Don't Cry, Daddy" and a great many other excellent songs, does most of his writing alone.

Chuck Berry, without whom rock and roll music would be infinitely poorer, composed some of the genre's greatest hits: "Johnny B. Good," "Sweet Little Sixteen," "Roll Over Beethoven," "School Days," "Maybelline," "Memphis, Tennessee" and many more. And he did it writing alone.

There are many writers who are self sufficient, those who can create songs of outstanding quality, songs that touch the heart and soul of listeners, songs that live on, day after day and year after year.

Many more could be mentioned, but perhaps the ultimate example of this type of songwriter is Irving Berlin. He wrote hundreds of songs, many that have become the standards by which all other songs are judged:

    𝄞   "Alexander's Ragtime Band"

    𝄞   "There's No Business Like Show Business"

    𝄞   "God Bless America"

♦   "Easter Parade"

♦   And the granddaddy of all popular songs, "White Christmas."

If your musical talents are not as broad, not as highly developed, or not as finely tuned as writers such as these, writing with a collaborator is probably a valid consideration.

Given the choice, you should co-write with someone who has more expertise than you. You might want to read the last part of that line again. The implication can be a bit tricky.

Simply put, it means that your co-writer should be a better writer than you, or be able to bring to the partnership an element of songwriting talent that you don't already possess. If he doesn't, you can't learn from him; he'll be learning from you.

Of course, if this line of reasoning is thought through, and strictly applied, everyone would have to write alone. No one would knowingly share his expertise with one whose talents he judged to be inferior to his own.

Writers usually get together to combine strengths rather than to offset weaknesses. There are exceptions, of course, but one writer will usually be the better lyricist, the other better with the music.

One of popular music's most famous songwriting teams was John Lennon and Paul McCartney. Together, they composed many of the songs that were hits for the Beatles.

Another famous songwriting team was Burt Bacharach and Hal David, who wrote hit songs for Dionne Warwick, B. J. Thomas, and countless others. They are no longer writing together, but during their co-writing stint they created many songs that set the standard of the day.

Jerry Leiber and Mike Stoller are another excellent example of co-writing success. During the fifties and sixties, these two young men wrote hits for everyone, from Elvis Presley on down. "Jailhouse Rock," "Treat Me Nice," and "Hound Dog" are only three of the songs they created for the man many called the King of Rock and Roll. They also enjoyed a great deal of success with the songs written for the Coasters: "Young Blood," "Searchin'," "Charlie Brown" and many others.

In the world of country music, the names of Felice and Boudleaux Bryant always come to mind when famous songwriting partners are mentioned. This husband and wife writing team blessed the music industry with numerous classics. "Bye Bye Love," "Wake Up Little Susie," and the song regarded by many to be the anthem of bluegrass music, the rousing "Rocky Top," are only a trio of the special songs created by this very special songwriting team.

But where mainstream country music is concerned, the most famous co-writing team of all time is Jerry Foster and Bill Rice. I know these two men quite well, and have since we were teenagers, when all of us were in the infancy of our music careers. I'm honored to call both my friends and it is a privilege to write of their accomplishments.

They are no longer writing together, but during almost a decade of collaboration, they penned over 1200 songs, 60% of which have been recorded. This is not only an awesome output of material but an equally high percentage of songs to be recorded.

Jerry and Bill, better known in the music industry as Foster and Rice, approached the craft of songwriting as a business — a business that had to be tended to each and every day. And their goal was to write a song every day. This was quite an ambitious undertaking, one that could not always be met. But it did not keep these two very talented writers from aiming for it and doing their best to fulfill it.

During their heydays, when the late William G. "Bill" Hall, their publisher, was at the helm of Hall-Clement Publications and Jack and Bill Music, Bill Rice and Jerry Foster wrote songs for almost all the top stars in country music. It would be simpler to list those who haven't recorded a Foster and Rice song than it would be to mention those who have. In many cases, it was a Foster and Rice song that rocketed a new artist to stardom.

Though their principle domain was Nashville and their goal was to fill the needs of the country music singer, their songs were recorded by artists in other fields as well — Sammy Davis Jr. and Robert Goulet, to mention only two.

In the late seventies, as though proving that all good things come to an end, Bill and Jerry went their separate ways. Individually, both are still making significant contributions to the music industry, but the team of Foster and Rice is no more. I wish them well, and, thank heavens, their music lives on.

Where co-writing is concerned, if you can go it alone, do so. If not, look for help.

It's as simple as that.

....
:   :
:   Chapter 13   :
:   :
....

Find Your Audience

Who are you writing for? If you're an amateur writer, one who dabbles at the craft for the enjoyment of it, the answer to this question is simple: You're writing for yourself. What you write, where you write, when you write, or how well you write is no one's business but yours. The results of your efforts will be enjoyed by you alone, so you can be as esoteric as you please.

But if you have plans to step up from the ranks of the amateurs to a more lofty perch, the luxuries cited above are luxuries that you can no longer afford. There are decisions to be made and realities to be faced.

One of the first things a writer must determine is who he's writing for. There are four main categories:

♦ Yourself, as an amateur

♦ Yourself, as a professional recording artist

♦ Other recording artists in general

♦ Other recording artists in particular

Yourself

In the beginning, you're writing for yourself, or simply because you have the urge to do so. Little or no thought is given to whether anyone else will like the song. And since songwriting is not your profession, considering the marketing of the song is also of no importance.

But when songwriting is your profession, or when you have made a commitment to try to become a professional, how your song will be marketed becomes the prime consideration.

Professional writers write for two reasons:

♦ To scratch the creative itch.

♦ To fill the needs of the market.

The second reason is more important. By doing it, the first reason is satisfied.

Yourself as a Professional Recording Artist

In many ways, this is an enviable position to be in. You know the extent of your talent, you know the direction of your career at the moment, you know in which direction you want it to go in the future, and you know your musical preferences. These are the pluses, and they're things that you know and understand better than anyone.

You can write for yourself and, as the artist, you know immediately whether the song is right for you. If you also happen to be your own producer, you know the song is going to be recorded. For a songwriter, this is about as good as it gets.

But there are two major drawbacks to this otherwise ideal situation: One is the awesome responsibility of being right in your judgment of the material. The other is finding the time to try to fill your song needs; having the time to write.

If you're an artist of any stature, if you're enjoying big-time success, there will be big-time demands on your time — time on the road performing, time spent being interviewed by radio and television personalities and reporters from magazines and newspapers. If you're really hot, more time will be consumed with television appearances as a performer and, of course, the filming of music videos. If you're married and have a family, still more time will have to be devoted to your spouse and children.

If all these demands are given their proper due, it's plain to see that there will be very little time left for songwriting.

There is one other very important thing that can be learned as you function as the writer of your own songs: You will learn to respect the needs of the customer.

For a moment, think of yourself as two people:

♦ Songwriter

♦ Recording artist.

As a songwriter, if you're like most songwriters, you want your song to be recorded. This is your need. The need of the recording artist is not yours. He's looking for a hit song, one that fits him like a three-piece suit tailored on Saville Row in London.

As the songwriter, you're the seller.

As the recording artist, he's the buyer — your customer. The customer may not always be right, but he's always the customer and he's paying the bills.

Please him, and you're on the road to success.

Writing for Other Recording Artists in General

This is another form of writing to please yourself, in that you are not being restricted by directing your efforts too precisely.

For the accomplished writer, the advantage of this method is that you can write your songs without paying a great deal of attention to the specific needs of the current market. You simply get a good idea and write the song as you think it should be written.

The disadvantage is that you will have to pay more attention to casting your songs than the writer who directs his efforts at only one target.

This method is: write the song, then find the artist.

If you live far away from one of the major recording centers, or have no strong ties to recording artists, producers, publishers, or other record label personnel, such as A & R men, this is probably the method you will have to use.

Writing for a Specific Artist

This method is: find the artist, then write the song.

If you live in or near one of the cities where a great deal of recording takes place: New York, Chicago, Detroit, Nashville, Atlanta, or Los Angeles, for example, this method of writing and placing songs will be a possibility. Your major responsibility, in addition to creating good songs, will be to keep a finger on the pulse of the business, to know who's recording, what kind of songs they're looking for, and when they need them.

If you plan to write for a specific artist, begin by doing your homework:

◆ What kind of song has he/she been recording?

◆ Have they ever deviated from this type of material? Is there a discernible pattern to the types of songs this artist records?

◆ Are more ballad songs recorded than uptempo ones?

◆ Is there some common thread running through the songs?

◆ If so, what is it?

There are many other questions that might be asked, but this gives you some idea of the kind of things the learning process might include.

Add to your knowledge by collecting information about the artists you're trying to write for. Start a file for each. If you hear something about a particular artist, write the information down and add it to his or her file. Again, don't rely on your memory. Some tidbit of information about this artist might inspire you to write his next smash hit. Magazines, newspapers, trade papers, and radio and television interviews are the other prominent places to look for information about this artist.

Try to get in tune with the artist's thinking or the image he has of himself. It would probably be futile to submit a sentimental ballad to an artist who's been recording hard-driving macho songs—unless you've learned that he's making a drastic change.

Don't try to reinvent the artist simply because you have a song you want him to record. He is what he is, and he is your customer.

Find out what he wants—help him get it—and you'll get what you want.

....

Chapter 14

....

All Through—What Now?

At one time or another, almost everyone has scribbled a few clever lines on a piece of paper, calling the results of their imaginative efforts one of two things: a poem or a song.

♦ A poem is words without music.

♦ A song is words with music.

Most people reach this point and go no further. Since neither songwriting nor poetry is their business, they enjoy a momentary feeling of satisfaction at having created something from nothing, but that's it. They stuff the paper into a drawer where such treasured things are kept and that's the end of their creative writing career.

It would interesting to know how many great songs have been written but have gone unheard by anyone other than the writer. The reason we've never heard them, in many instances, is that the writer had no idea what to do next. And he was afraid to ask, or perhaps he was embarrassed to admit that he didn't know.

Throughout the course of this book, the various facets of the songwriting process have been compared to the links of a chain. To do so again seems appropriate. All the links are important, all have to be strong, and all have to be in place if everything is to hold together.

Each succeeding link in the songwriting chain is just as important as the one that came before it. You've written a song and, by all appearances, it's a good one.

Now what? Do you stuff it in the drawer or do you take the next step? If the latter half of the question is your reply, there are a number of things remaining to be done. Preparing and assembling the various parts of your submission is one.

Lyric Sheets

When your song is truly finished, after all the revising, rewriting and polishing has been done, it's time to prepare a master copy of the lyrics.

The rule here is simple: Lyric sheets should be typed and they should be perfect. If a word is misspelled, correct it. Use plain white paper, with double spaces between the lines, and with nothing on the page but the following: your title, the words of your song, and your name as the composer. Anything else will divert attention away from your song and you can't afford that. If you expect your work to be taken seriously, you must take it seriously.

Presentation is as important as content. The more professional the presentation, the more attention the content will be given.

Demos

There was a time when most demonstration tapes consisted of nothing more than a single voice and a single instrument, usually voice and guitar or voice and piano. This should still be sufficient to display the major aspects of your song. Unfortunately, in many cases, it isn't.

One instance where a more elaborate demo might be required is when your song is a bit more complicated than the average song. Perhaps a certain musical riff plays a vital role. If this is the case, do what has to be done to properly showcase the song. If another instrument is needed, use it. If a full band is needed, use it. Don't be more extravagant than you have to be, but don't scrimp in the wrong places. Here, let the song's needs be your guide.

Whatever is required, do it, and do it well. If your strength is in writing and not in singing, hire someone to sing the song for you. Even if your demo is nothing more than a single voice with one instrument, be sure that both perform properly. No mistakes. Again, as it is with lyric sheets, mistakes will divert the attention of your listener.

Home recording is very popular today, especially with songwriters. If your home recording equipment produces a clean, clear sound, use it. If not, use a professional recording studio. A good, clean recording of your song is part of your presentation. Make listening to your song a pleasant experience. Even if the song you're pitching is not accepted for recording at this particular time, a professional presentation will ensure that it will be listened to on another day. Opening the door is one thing, staying inside is another.

The second reason that a single voice/single instrument demo might not be adequate has to do with the person you're pitching the song to, whether it's a publisher, producer, or recording artist.

There are still those in the music business who can listen to a simple voice/instrument demonstration tape and imagine how the drums, the bass, and all the other instruments will sound. But there are also those who have very little imagination. For them, a more elaborate demo might be required, one where all the parts of your song and its arrangement are fully demonstrated.

To determine how complex your demos will have to be, become familiar with the expectations or requirements of your buyer. There is no one rule to follow, so do your homework. Here, let your buyer's needs be your guide.

Note: Almost all demo tapes today are cassettes. Again, don't scrimp. Use a quality name brand tape. Ideally, use custom length cassettes, perhaps C-10, 5 minutes per side. This will allow you to put one song on each side of the tape, and one song per side makes it easy to listen to. It also makes it easy to rewind and listen again.

Cover Letters

Having the opportunity of sitting across the desk from a publisher, a producer, or a recording artist as the person listens to your song is a rare luxury, one that might not ever come your way. Even if you live near a major recording center and deliver your songs to the potential buyer in person, the tape will rarely be listened to at that moment.

This being true, the importance of cover letters becomes clear. As with your lyric sheets and your tapes, your cover letter should further display your professional approach to your business.

To begin, use standard business letterheads and envelopes. Any designs or frills on your stationary should enhance the appearance of your submission, not detract from it. This is a business meeting, not a birthday party.

In your cover letter, stick to the facts. A few things to be mentioned are:

♦ Why you're submitting your material. Perhaps it is as a result of seeing a listing in a trade paper or on a tip sheet.

♦ How many songs you're submitting. (3 maximum)

♦ Which recording artist the songs are written for.

♦ That you've enclosed a self-addressed stamped envelope (SASE), for return of the material if it's not acceptable. (For submitting cassettes, use a 6" X 9" brown or white envelope or something comparable. Use another for your SASE.)

To these bare facts, add a thank you for considering your songs, then say goodbye. Don't mention your needs, your experience, your Aunt Minnie or your cousin Wilbur. And don't tell how good the songs are; they will speak for themselves. If they don't, you still have work to do.

Compare the way you present your songs to the way you dress when you attend an important business meeting, perhaps with your banker when you're arranging a loan.

First impressions are important. You can't afford to be sloppy or cute — unless you can afford to fail.

You can only take liberties with friends. If the person you're presenting your song to is not yet a friend, mind your manners.

```
. . . . . . . . . . . . . . . . . . . .
:                                      :
:          Chapter 15                  :
:                                      :
. . . . . . . . . . . . . . . . . . . .
```

Publishers

What are they? What do they do? What are they looking for?

At first glance, songwriters who are new to the craft will probably be more interested in the third question than the first or second. But to better understand what a publisher is looking for, knowing what they are, and what they do will prepare you to deal with the third.

What Are They?

Other than the various legal aspects of copyrights, the role played by a music publisher is probably the one area of the music business that is the most vague, confusing, or misunderstood. Simply defined, a publisher is one who reproduces copies of something and distributes them for sale.

A publisher was once someone who dealt only in printed material: newspapers, magazines or books. In the early days of the music industry, a music publisher

114 Songwriting: From Ideas to Royalties

duplicated and distributed sheet music and songbooks.

For example, John Stark, the copyright owner and publisher of many of the songs of Scott Joplin—the legendary king of ragtime—had but few options available to him. His usual procedure was to duplicate a piece of sheet music and to have the song performed in his music store so potential buyers could hear how it sounded. Another option was to present copies of the sheet music to the vocalists of the day, many of whom performed on stage as members of a touring company and still others who plied their vocal wares on riverboats, or "showboats," as they were sometimes called.

With the advent of recorded sound, the music publisher saw his copyrighted works duplicated on piano rolls and records, and then synchronized with motion picture film.

The publisher of today enjoys many more options. He might see his music printed in songbooks and sheet music, recorded and released on tapes, vinyl records and compact discs, and recorded on videotape or film for use in television or in the movies. Portions of his songs might also be used in radio and television commercials. And all this is in addition to live public performances in nightclubs, hotel showrooms, bars, restaurants and other venues.

Publishers come in all sizes. A publisher might be an individual with a solely-owned company holding the rights to only a few songs. A publisher might also be a partnership, or it might be a giant corporation, perhaps one holding the copyrights to thousands of songs. The size of the company, to some extent, is unimportant. The excellence of his material is what counts.

What Do They Do?

Publishers acquire the publishing rights to songs from songwriters. They usually do this by issuing a contract to the writer, an agreement containing clauses describing the role the publisher will play and clauses listing what is expected of the writer. In signing this contract, the writer also grants to the publisher the right to register the copyright for the song. In most cases, the copyright will be registered in the name of the publishing company as the owner of exclusive rights and in the name of the writer as the creator of the work, as the song is referred to on the copyright registration form.

There are three basic ways publishers acquire songs:

- ◆ Staff writers

- ◆ Subpublishing agreements with foreign publishers

- ◆ Freelance writers

Normally, staff writers are writers who are under exclusive contract to write for one publisher. For this privilege, the publisher usually pays the writer a draw; an advance against future royalties earned by the writer's songs. As a normal rule, this draw is paid every week, and the amount will depend on how valuable the writer is to the publisher and the amount of royalties his songs are earning or are expected to earn.

Subpublishing agreements are agreements made between the publishers of two different countries, the United States and Great Britain for instance. These agreements will be of little interest to most writers, unless he is the creator of one of the works involved in such an arrangement.

The other source of acquiring songs is from freelance writers. For the writer, this role affords more freedom and allows him the opportunity to place his songs in many areas and with many publishers. For the freelance writer, however, there is usually no advance financial consideration, such as being paid a draw against future royalties.

The roles played by today's publisher are much more varied and complex than the publishers of yesteryear. Rather than simply acquiring songs from writers and attempting to match those songs with the appropriate recording artist, the publisher of today might also have a hand in the development of recording artists as well as songwriters.

A publisher might also bring writers together, perhaps in hopes of pairing the songwriting superstars of tomorrow. These and many other options might be performed in addition to the traditional publisher's role of securing copyright protection and overseeing the administration of the company's catalog.

There are those publishers who are the holders of song copyrights and little more. For the writer, with hopes of finding the perfect publisher, one who will aggressively exploit his material, some homework will be required.

A good place to begin to inquire about a publisher would be one of the three performing rights societies.

 ♦ BMI – (Broadcast Music, Inc.)

 ♦ ASCAP – (American Society of Composers, Authors, Publishers)

♦   SESAC, Inc. – (Selected Editions of Standard
American Catalogues)

(Addresses and phone numbers for these
organizations will be found in the organization section.)
All U. S. publishers will be affiliated with one of
these performing rights organizations. If a publisher
has subsidiaries, he might be affiliated with all of them.

Determine which society your prospective
publisher is affiliated with. This information will be
found on sheet music, in songbooks, and possibly on
record labels or album jackets. Call the publisher's
performing rights organization and ask a few questions.
They won't be able to tell you everything about a
publisher, of course, but they should be able to tell you
enough to give you some idea about the reputation of
the company in question.

What Are They Looking For?

The simplest answer to this question is: a hit song.
The reply is the truth; every music publisher in the
world is looking for a hit song. Unfortunately, this
reply is a bit too vague and too general to be of much
help to a songwriter, either beginning or professional.

The needs of the publisher might vary, depending
on the focus of his attention. There are publishers who
publish nothing but religious or gospel music. Others
might not be so specific, but they will have categories
of the music industry where their contacts will be
stronger in one genre than another.

Though Nashville is the home of the Grand Ole
Opry, and is world famous for the recording of country
music, there is much more to the city's music activity
than that. Artists from every field of music have been

known to try the waters of Nashville at one time or another. As a consequence, Nashville publishers acquire a wide variety of music for their catalogs.

At the present time, New York, Los Angeles and Nashville are the nation's three most successful music capitals. Though they all have their specialties, the needs of publishers in these cities will be quite varied. No matter what you write, if it's good, the top is always the target to aim for.

There is one major obstacle to breaking into the major markets, Nashville, for example. If you don't live there, your greatest challenge will be to find an open door. The demand for a friendly ear has placed a strain on many in the industry. With the increase in popularity of country music, the input of songs into this market has greatly increased. Unfortunately, the quality of some of the material has been lacking. As a consequence, more and more doors have been closed to those songwriters who are unknown to the more prominent producers and publishers.

(Coping with a situation such as this will be addressed in Chapter 16: Contacts.)

As a writer, you are trying to write a fresh song, one that says something in an unusual way, one that will be in step with today's market or perhaps even a step ahead. The music publisher — whether the company is small, medium or large — is looking for the same thing.

There appears to be nothing new to write about, or at least nothing of any great interest to the masses. Your hope, as a writer, is that you can think of a different way to say the things that have already been said. If you can do that, with style and flare, there will be a publisher who wants to hear from you.

....
:   :
:   **Chapter 16**   :
:   :
....

Contacts

Songs are like any other product — they have to be researched, developed, and marketed. The way to do this is the same way you would do with any other business — begin where you are.

In marketing your song, you are a salesperson. To make the sale, you have to make the calls.

A good way to begin is to investigate the music business in your hometown. If you live in or near one of the nation's recording capitals, this chore will be relatively easy. There will be lots of activity, lots of choices, and plenty of possibilities for placing your songs. If you live somewhere else, as most people do, a bit more effort will be required.

If you write gospel or religious music, for example, begin by learning about the gospel singing groups in your town, then in the surrounding area. Watch your newspaper for announcements or ads telling about the groups that will be appearing at churches or auditoriums or perhaps at a singing convention. Again, you are a salesman; you have to make the call. Find out if these groups have plans to record and, if so, if they are now choosing their material.

Don't be intimidated if someone in your town or someone who lives close to you has become nationally known. Everyone is a local boy/girl somewhere. (Though it seems rather ridiculous, there were a few people in Memphis who considered Elvis Presley nothing more than a local boy.)

In your town, or perhaps in a town nearby, you might have the opportunity to place a song with one of the nation's top singing groups. Look upon this as a golden opportunity. If your songs are truly good, they're good enough for anyone, and these are the people you're looking for.

Make Your Presentation Properly

Make your presentation properly. Don't go to an auditorium and thrust tapes and lyric sheets at anyone. Find out the name of the leader of the group or the name of the person to whom songs should be submitted. Introduce yourself, if and when the opportunity presents itself, and state that you are a songwriter and that you would like to submit material.

You won't be able to impress anyone by telling them how good your songs are, so don't try. Give the person one of your business cards and get one of his. You have to know how to get in touch, so don't go away empty-handed, even if this person has to write on the back of one of your cards.

In addition to establishing as many contacts as possible, make an effort to become better known within the music business community. Have plenty of business cards and place them in the right hands as you make your rounds. Make getting in touch with you the easiest thing in the world.

Above all, always conduct yourself in a professional manner. Do so and you can expect your songs to be treated in kind.

If you write country, rock and roll or popular music, the details of establishing yourself will vary from the example above, but the procedure will be much the same. Again, begin by becoming familiar with the recording activity in your area; become a part of it. Develop some expertise in presenting your material, then branch out, just as you would with any other business.

Rejection

Although it should be well known by now, there's one other very important thing to remember here. As it is with all salesmen, rejection is a fact of life. Not everyone you call on will buy something. As a general rule, if they don't need it, they won't buy it. If you get a song turned down, don't take it personally. Your work is being rejected, not you. And the rejection might not be because of the quality of your work. It might be that it is just not right for this particular artist or perhaps does not fit the direction this artist is going at this particular time.

If you can't sell the song, sell yourself. Be courteous, well-mannered, pleasant and professional in your demeanor and attitude. You may have to bite your lip to do so, but do it. There will be another day and another song.

Be prepared, be patient, be persistent. These things will open many doors.

Who You Know

The following is not to be construed as a negative statement, but a very important factor in being successful in any field of endeavor is who you know; who will open their door; who will give your song an honest listen.

Walk up to a friend's house and knock on the door. When they recognize you, the door will be opened.

Now, walk up to a stranger's door and see what happens.

Prepare, Then Look for Opportunity

Write your songs, then look for the chance to place them. Look for those open doors.

Any salesman will tell you that it's easier to sell to friends than to strangers. So get out and make friends within the music business community. You can have the greatest songs in the world and they can still go unheard if there's no one to hear them.

Begin where you are, then expand. This expansion can begin by asking yourself a few simple questions:

♦ Who do I know at a major record label?

♦ Who do I know at a major publishing company?

♦ Is one of my friends now a famous recording artist?

♦ Is one of my friends now a noted record producer?

- Is one of my friends an A & R man or promotion man?

- Keep asking similar questions until you get a favorable reply.

Is there someone you know who is on a higher rung on the music business ladder than you?

If the answer is yes, then make some attempt to use this friendship/relationship to open a door. This is taking advantage of a situation but it is not to be regarded as an unfair one. If you have something good to offer, your friend, or whoever this person might be, will be glad to hear from you.

Look for the open door.

If your songs are good, you'll be able to get inside and stay inside.

Chapter 17

Copyrights

This facet of the business of songwriting is undoubtedly the one most misunderstood by the beginning songwriter and the general public. The moment someone scribbles 12 or 16 lines on a piece of paper, they begin to think "copyright." But they have absolutely no idea what it means.

Another interesting thing happens once those twelve or sixteen lines have been completed. The writer of those lines immediately becomes suspicious, thinking that everyone in the world is going to try to steal his song.

This sudden change in attitude is amazing for a number of reasons.

1. How and when did this transformation take place? A moment ago, everyone was OK. They were honest and trustworthy, as most people are. But now that you've written some words on a piece of paper, a few of the words even rhyming, everyone in the world is a crook. How did this happen?

2. If what you've written is indeed a song, or bears some resemblance to a song, what makes you think it's worth stealing? Unless you're a professional songwriter, the excellence of the material has to be questioned, at least to some degree. Hardly anyone writes a perfect song on the first attempt.

3. If you have indeed created something special and desirable, no one knows that the copyright is not registered but you. And they won't know until you tell them.

4. If you have indeed created something of value, then deal with reputable people, those who are in the business to do business, those who plan to stay in business. If your song is good, a reputable person wouldn't steal it; he will probably want to use it as it is. If it isn't any good, it isn't worth stealing.

The First Misconception

The first misconception about copyrights concerns how and when they begin. Simply stated, your copyrights begin the moment you lift your pencil from the paper. You're the creator of the work, you're the copyright owner, and the law says the song is yours to do with as you please.

To make it legal, at the bottom of the first page of your song, do one of the following, using the current year and your name:

Copyright © 2000 John Q. Doe

Copyright 2000 John Q. Doe

© 2000 John Q. Doe

Your song is copyrighted at that moment and any one of the three forms of copyright notices above are acceptable.

The Second Misconception

The second misconception concerns registering a copyright. You can mail a copy of the words and music of your song to yourself, or a tape recording, and not open the letter or package. This proves that on that day that song existed in that form. This procedure has held up in court, but it has also been defeated. If your song is worth anything, and having it registered would make you feel more comfortable, then by all means register it.

There is only one perfectly legal way to register the copyright to your song and that is with the register of copyrights in Washington D. C.

Rather than take up time and space reproducing all the details of the copyright laws, for complete information write:

Register of Copyrights
Library of Congress
Washington, D. C. 20559

Ask for information booklets about copyrights and, if you have completed songs that you feel you should register, request a supply of form PA.

This form can be used to register a song as a published or an unpublished work. A writer might register the song as an unpublished work, meaning that copies of the work have not been formally distributed. When the song is placed with a publishing company, the publisher has to register the song again, but now as a published work, meaning that copies of the work have been distributed.

To properly register the song, copies of the work must be deposited with the Register of Copyrights. This may be done in the form of a lead sheet; a sheet illustrating words and melody, or in a tape recording.

The current registration fee is $30.00 per song.

Unless a song has been recorded and released on record, registering a song ahead of time, in most cases, is a waste of time and money. Again, do business with reputable people and companies. Do this and many of your worries and fears concerning copyrights can be allayed, leaving you more time to do what you really should be doing — writing songs!

The Third Area of Concern

The third area of concern to a writer is the duration of a copyright.

As of March 25, 1998, a copyright is good for the author's life plus seventy years. At the end of that time the song falls into "Public Domain." This means that the song can be recorded by anyone, but with no one paying for the use of it. As the author, you will probably still be listed as such, however, no royalties have to be paid to your heirs for the use of your song.

Between 1909 and December 31, 1977, songs could be copyrighted for 28 years. At the end of the initial 28 years, the copyright could be renewed for an additional 28 years. The renewal was not automatic and it is not automatic today. For songs copyrighted prior to January 1, 1978, if you desire to renew them, the renewal form RE must be filed during the final year of the initial copyright period. Again, forms for renewal may be obtained by writing the Register of Copyrights and requesting a supply of form RE.

Another Area of Concern

Another area of concern to a beginning songwriter is — what is copyrightable? It's probably simpler to list what can't be copyrighted. The areas of major concern are listed below.

Titles

Titles cannot be copyrighted. The exception here is a title that has become so well known that it would seem to be an obvious attempt to infringe if it were used. You can write a song entitled "White Christmas" if you want to, but don't expect the title to be approved.

You also cannot copyright a chord progression. To be considered an original, copyrightable work, your song must have melody and rhythm.

Concepts

You cannot copyright a concept. If concepts could be copyrighted, we would have only one song in each possible category. There would only be one song about love, for instance.

How Much Is Infringement?

There is no specified number of notes that you can use from another song before it becomes infringement. Legal action has been brought and won on as few as three notes. If you are aware that the melody of your song sounds like another song, change yours.

The Last Misconception

Finally, the last misconception is the idea that by registering your song with the Register of Copyrights that you have proof that it is original or that you have a valid claim. This is not true. When your song is registered, it is simply being put on file at the Library of Congress. The Register of Copyrights makes no search or comparison to determine whether your song infringes on the copyright of a previously registered song.

Note: The two most valuable song copyrights in the world are: "White Christmas" & "Rudolph The Red Nosed Reindeer."

Chapter 18

Royalties

Of all the possible reasons that might be given for doing something, there are only three of any real consequence: Fun, Love, and Money. When survival is eliminated from consideration, most human activity will be motivated by one or more of these. This is also true for the songwriter.

You May Begin for Fun

If you're like most people, you begin writing songs for the fun of it, because you have a knack for putting words on paper, making them rhyme and setting them to a melody. If you write long enough, if you're honestly trying to learn and you're using that knowledge to improve your skills, you'll probably get good at it. You might even get very good at it.

Then You Perform

When you reach that point, when you've developed some expertise, you will eventually begin to make some effort to share your songs with others, perhaps even the world. To do that, your songs will have to be performed by utilizing one of the mass media systems: radio or television. Better yet, they will be recorded, preserved for all time, to be enjoyed today, tomorrow, and always.

Jimmie Rodgers and Hank Williams are gone. Buddy Holly, Sam Cooke, Jim Croce, and Jackie Wilson are gone. Patsy Cline, Janis Joplin, and Dottie West are gone. And, like so many more of our musical favorites, Elvis is gone, too. But, through their music, these legendary performers live on.

A few of these artists wrote their own songs, but much of their music was created by others. And through these recordings, the artists not only live on but the songwriters continue to generate income — royalties, the fruit of the songwriter's labor — money, the third of the three principal reasons most human beings do things.

Music and Technology

The technology that enabled music to be recorded also made it possible for there to be substantial royalties. Before recorded music, many songwriters sold their songs outright, as a painting might be sold.

While others might not sell them, their choices of ways their songs could be displayed were few. The writer's songs might be performed by members of a minstrel troupe, a popular show business forum of the day, or perhaps be reproduced in sheet music or song books. Even in these two latter forms, the royalties were pitifully small at times. America was struggling to survive, times were hard, and luxuries were few.

Stephen Foster

One of the most famous songwriters in the history of American music is Stephen Foster. His story is also one of the more tragic.

Stephen Collins Foster was born in Lawrenceville, Pennsylvania (now part of Pittsburgh) on July 4, 1826. He died in the charity ward of Bellevue Hospital in New York City on January 13, 1864. He was thirty-seven years old and it's reported that he had little more than that many pennies in his pocket.

But between the sunrise and sunset of his life, he had established himself as the premier songwriter of his day. A few of his more memorable songs are "Old Black Joe," "Camptown Races," "Jeanie with the Light Brown Hair," "Oh! Susanna," and "Old Folks at Home."

Of the more than two hundred songs written by this sensitive, sentimental writer, the hauntingly beautiful "My Old Kentucky Home" has come to be considered his masterpiece. The song will live forever, if but for one reason — the playing and singing of this lilting melody as the thoroughbred horses parade to the post on the first Saturday in May at Churchill Downs in Louisville, Kentucky. As long as this horse race endures — the equally famous Kentucky Derby — the music of Stephen Foster will not be forgotten.

Opportunities Are Great

The opportunities for the songwriter of today, thank heaven, are much greater than those enjoyed by Stephen Foster. And though the financial opportunities of his day were few, the demand for excellence in the creative sense was great. And that demand is no less today. The good song is still the one that generates the most royalties.

Royalty Sources

Mechanical Royalties

These are royalties for record sales — fees paid by a record company for the use of a song in all the present configurations of recorded music. The mechanical royalty rate is a part of the copyright law and the present rate was set by the Copyright Royalty Tribunal. (The Copyright Royalty Tribunal was dissolved on December 17, 1993, by legislation signed by President Clinton. Future royalty rate adjustments will be determined by an arbitration panel operating under the jurisdiction of the U. S. Copyright Office and the Library of Congress.)

As of January 1, 2000, the mechanical royalty rate was slightly over seven and a half cents (7.55 cents) per song for each copy made and distributed, or almost one and one-half cents (1.45 cents) for each minute of playing time per song, whichever total is greater. This rate applies to sales in all the current popular configurations — cassettes, vinyl records and compact discs. Although subject to earlier revision, this rate is expected to be in effect for the next two years. (The next scheduled rate increase, to 8.0 cents per song or 1.55 cents per minute, whichever total is greater, is due to take effect on January 1, 2002.)

The arbitration panel mentioned above will determine future rate changes and the period of time for which the rates will be in effect.

The normal procedure is for mechanical royalties to be divided equally between the publisher and the songwriter. This is regarded as the standard division of this royalty. Check your songwriter's contract if this is not true in your case.

Sheet Music and Song Books

The royalty rate to be paid to the songwriter for the use of his song in sheet music and songbook form will be set forth in a clause of the publisher's contract. These rates are set by the publisher and they vary from publisher to publisher. Sheet music royalties are usually paid on the number of copies actually sold. Compensation for the privilege of reproducing your song in a songbook is usually a flat fee agreed upon by the publisher.

Movie Synchronization

The fees to be paid for using a song in a movie are negotiated by the publisher, on his and the songwriter's behalf. Royalties are usually divided equally between publisher and writer.

Public Performance

Royalties for public performances of a writer's songs are normally collected through his affiliation with one of the performing rights organizations: BMI, ASCAP, SESAC. These organizations, or societies, as they are sometimes called, acquire rights from songwriters and publishers and in turn grant licenses to use its entire repertoire to users of music.

For example, BMI collects fees from each user of music they license and distribute to their writers and publishers all the money collected, other than what is needed for operating expenses. The songwriter and his publisher have individual agreements with the same licensing organization, and each is paid individually. Statements, and any royalties earned, are usually tendered four (4) times a year, approximately quarterly.

There are more than 75,000 establishments in the United States where music is performed. A few of the more popular places where your songs might be used are radio and television stations, nightclubs, hotels, amusement parks, and sports stadiums. There are many others, ranging from high school auditoriums to the Broadway stage, but the importance of these licensing organizations is apparent. It would be virtually impossible for an individual to monitor all these music users himself or to collect the fees for the use of his songs.

The normal time to affiliate with a performing rights organization is when you have a song released on record. Again, writer and publisher will belong to the same organization.

At BMI, there is no affiliation fee for the songwriter and only an initial $150.00 fee for individually owned publishing companies and a $250.00 fee for partnerships, corporations, and limited liability companies to help defray administrative costs. Neither writer nor publisher pays a yearly fee.

At ASCAP, there is no initiation fee, but annual dues are $10.00 for writers and $50.00 for publishers.

At SESAC, there is no fee for affiliation or annual fees.

A Recap

Briefly and simply, this is where the money comes from, how it is paid, and by whom. As you can see, songwriters make their money a few cents at a time. But it soon adds up.

The distance between ideas and royalties can be very far, but there's a good way to get there, and the journey can be quite pleasant. Come up with a good idea, a good title, a good opening line, then build on it.

Chapter 19

Bits and Pieces

More often than not, failure can be traced to the strength of our words rather than the weakness of our efforts. Simply put, we talk ourselves out of succeeding. We tell ourselves that we can't do something — and we believe it!

The 3 D's of Success

Songwriting differs very little from other fields of human endeavor. To succeed at anything, there must be desire, direction and determination. Bits and pieces of other ingredients might be mixed in, but these three things are the foundation of all achievement.

- ◆ Desire: What do you want?

- ◆ Direction: How are you going to get it?

- ◆ Determination: How long and how hard are you willing to work to get it?

If you ask these three questions, and answer them, you can be on your way toward success, in songwriting or in any profession you choose.

Desire: What Do You Want?

If you have the desire to do something, and if that desire is so strong that you can taste it, you will begin to take the steps to do something about it. And don't worry. You will not have any desire that you cannot fulfill. If you honestly and truly do not have the ability to do something, any desire that you might have had will soon go away.

But the contest should be decided in a fair fight. The desire to do something should be defeated by unsuccessful physical efforts rather than by dissuasive oratory.

If you're going to talk, it's better to talk yourself into doing something rather than talking yourself out of it. Think of all the reasons something can be done instead of the reasons that it can't.

By all the usual standards of measurement, Spud Webb and Tyrone Bogues should not be playing basketball in the NBA. Webb is 5' 7" and Bogues is only 5' 5". Someone obviously forgot to tell these men of modest stature about how things are done in big league basketball, the land of towering giants, where most players are six and a half feet tall or more and where a few are even over seven feet tall.

Not Taking No for an Answer

Webb and Bogues, by all the normal expectations, should be doing something other than what they're doing. But these two men are excellent examples of not taking NO for an answer. They've undoubtedly been told that they're crazy, or at least foolish, for ever entertaining such an idea as actually playing in the NBA.

But the desire to do so was obviously so strong that they closed their ears to all the discouraging words. Especially Spud Webb. He's a former winner of the NBA Slam Dunk Contest. How's that for thumbing your nose at all the usual expectations?

Jim Abbott is another professional athlete who doesn't take NO for an answer. He first distinguished himself as an outstanding baseball pitcher during the 1988 Olympic Games. He then went on to pitch for the California Angels in the Western Division of the American League.

Jim has a physical handicap, a serious one for a man with big league baseball aspirations. He has but one hand. He has every right to be doing something else. No one would have expected more of him.

But the lowly expectations of others were of no concern to this courageous young man. His desire was great, and with only one limb he's made more of a mark on the world than many people ever do with two.

Kristi Yamaguchi

A more recent example of the power of unquench-able desire is the story of Kristi Yamaguchi, the charming, young figure skating Gold Medal winner in the 1992 Winter Olympics.

Born with badly deformed feet, Kristi wore casts for 9 months and learned to walk with bars and corrective shoes. She started ice skating as a form of therapy. But therapy soon gave birth to something more — a dream. Her dream was to be a champion. She is!

These are but three fine examples of not only having great desires but overcoming seemingly insurmountable odds to fulfill those desires. Most of us do not have to labor under anything approaching these circumstances.

Direction: Getting What You Want

This is where you decide how you're going to begin to fulfill your desires. Desire is the WANT TO. Direction is the HOW TO.

List Your Strengths

A good place to begin is by listing your strengths — taking stock of all the things that will assist you in reaching your goal.

In songwriting, as it is in life in general, a broad knowledge of your language is a great advantage. This gives you the opportunity to pick and choose the words you will use to say the things you want to say. The more words you know, the more choices you have. The more choices you have, the better you can express yourself.

For instance, you've written a line where you've used the word "remember." This word has three syllables. But you've decided that a shorter word would be a little better, snappier, and more suited to your purpose. It isn't a rhyming word at the end of a line, so your only concern is with the meaning.

How about "recall?" Recall means to remember and has only two syllables. This is but one small example, but it perfectly illustrates the advantage of knowing your language.

Imagination

Imagination is another desirable trait. Imagining things that have never been—and perhaps never will be—but writing about them, and making them all seem real, is a rare talent.

Musical Ability

In songwriting, some knowledge of musical instruments is obviously preferable. Having a way with words as well as having some knowledge of music will allow you to write alone.

Begin by fully using the talents you already have. Use them in the proper way, then proceed by striving to add to those talents. If you're trying, you'll probably be improving. If you're improving, you're one step closer to your goal. And if you can see your goal, you know you're moving in the right direction.

Determination: Working to Get What You Want

Determination is nothing more than persistence; it's finishing the things you begin. But this is where most people give up.

You're on the road toward your goal, and you're in the vehicle that will take you there. But you get weary. Impatience gets in and you get out.

Desire is easy. Desire is the WANT TO, and, as humans, we're filled with a lot of that.

Direction is the HOW TO, and it's a little more difficult. Discovering the proper direction takes some thought, some effort, some work. Work is a four -letter word and there are those who avoid it like the plague. But to succeed, you must have a plan. It might be simple, but it's still a plan.

Determination is the WILL DO, the last of the 3 D's of success. It's the last mountain to be climbed. On the other side is the land of golden opportunity — where the grass is green, the water is cool, and the air is fresh and clean. Over this mountain is where boys become men and girls become women. This is also where the ordinary man becomes a hero.

Two Choices

For those who can take one more step, there are great rewards. For those who quit....you'll find them sitting on the sidelines, watching.

Remember, there are only two ways to live your life: in the game or in the bleachers. The choice is yours.

A FEW REMINDERS AND OTHER THINGS

♦ If you like the work you're doing, you have a career.

♦ If you don't like the work you're doing, you have a job.

♦ Most people don't plan to fail, they fail to plan.

♦ Success: The progressive realization of a worthy goal.

♦ If you'll settle for less, that's usually what you'll get.

♦ Your only limitation:

♦ The size of your ideas and the degree of your dedication.

♦ Keep stars in your eyes and your feet on the ground.

♦ Time is the money of life; spend it wisely.

♦ Q: How long does it take to write a song?
A: Your lifetime plus 20 minutes.

♦ Mix reality with aspirations.

♦ Think positively. Find a way to reach your goals.

♦ Your mind: Use it or lose it.

♦ To find diamonds, you have to move rocks.

♦ A hero is no braver than anyone else. He merely fought a minute longer.

♦ Strive for quality, not quantity.

♦ "Gone With The Wind" was Margaret Mitchell's only book.

♦ Write with a pencil. The first words you choose may not be your last.

♦ Don't fall in love with anything you put on the page. It may have to be changed.

♦ Writing does not get easier, it just gets more familiar.

♦ If there was no one left but you, could you do the job?

♦ Q: What is luck?
A: When preparation meets opportunity.

♦ Failing is not a crime; not trying is.

♦ Do your best!

♦ Have fun!

♦ Play to win!

....
:   :
:   Chapter 20   :
:   :
....

Organizations

Performing Rights Societies

BMI - (Broadcast Music Inc.)
320 West 57th Street
New York, N. Y. 10019
212-586-2000
Fax: 212-245-8986
     -also-
BMI
10 Music Square East
Nashville, Tenn. 37203
615-291-6700
Fax: 615-291-6707

BMI
8730 Sunset Blvd.
Los Angeles, Calif. 90069
310-659-9109
Fax: 310-657-6947

BMI
79 Harley House
Marylebone Road
London NW1 5HN
England
011-4471-935-8517
Fax: 011-4471-487-5091

ASCAP - (American Society of Composers, Authors,
Publishers)
One Lincoln Plaza
New York, N. Y. 10019
212-595-3050
    -also-
ASCAP
66 Music Square West
Nashville, Tenn. 37203
615-320-1211

SESAC, Inc. - (Selected Editions of Standard American
Catalogues)
10 Columbus Circle
New York, N. Y. 10019
212-586-1708
    -also-
SESAC
55 Music Square East
Nashville, Tenn. 37203
615-320-0055

Mechanical Rights Representative:
The Harry Fox Agency
711 Third Avenue
New York, N. Y. 10017
212-834-0150

(The Harry Fox Agency represents most of the major U. S. publishers in granting mechanical and synchronization licenses and collecting fees for them from the record companies and producers who need them.)

Other Music Associations

Academy of Country Music
6255 Sunset Blvd. Ste. 923
Hollywood, Calif. 90028
213-462-2351

CMA (Country Music Association)
1 Music Circle South
Nashville, Tenn. 37203
615-244-2840

GMA (Gospel Music Association)
P. 0. Box 23201
Nashville, Tenn. 37202
615-242-0303
Fax: 615-254-9755

International Bluegrass Music Association
326 St. Elizabeth Street
Owensboro, Ky. 42301
502-684-9025

The Dramatists Guild, Inc.
234 West 44th Street
New York, N. Y. 10036
212-398-9366

NSAI (Nashville Songwriters Association, International)
803 Eighteenth Avenue South
Nashville, Tenn. 37203
615-321-5004

The Songwriters Guild
276 Fifth Avenue
New York, N. Y. 10001
212-686-6820

NARAS (National Academy of Recording Arts and
Sciences)
303 North Glenoaks Blvd.
Suite 140
Burbank, Calif. 91502
213-849-1313
Fax: 213-849-2529
(NARAS presents Grammy Awards annually)

Unions

A F of M (American Federation of Musicians)
304 East 44th Street
New York, N. Y. 10017
212-551-1200

Copyrights

Register of Copyrights
Library of Congress
Washington, D. C. 20559
202-479-0700

Chapter 21

Credits and Permissions

"Grandma Got Run Over by a Reindeer" – p. 24
(R. Brooks)

"Don't Start Something You Can't Finish" – p. 29–56
(Joe Keene)
Joe Keene Music Co. BMI

"There's More Where that Came From" – p. 30
(Joe Keene)
Lincoln Road Music Co. BMI

"Stardust" – p. 30
(Hoagy Carmichael-Mitchell Parrish)
Mills Music, Inc. ASCAP

"Mood Indigo " – p. 30
(Ellington/Mills/Bigard)
Mills Music, Inc. ASCAP

"Laura" – p. 30
(J. Mercer-D. Raskin)

"Marie" – p. 30
(Irving Berlin)

"Peggy Sue" – p. 30
(Allison/Petty/Holly)
Melody Lane Publ. Inc. BMI

"I've Just Found Another Reason For Loving You" –
p. 32
(Joe Keene–Charles Isbell)
Pi-Gem Music, BMI

"Doctor Love" – p. 33/34
(Joe Keene)
Lincoln Road Music Co. BMI

"I Got You (I Feel Good)" – p. 44
(James Brown)
Lois Music/Try Me Music, BMI

"The Most Beautiful Girl in the World" – p. 44
(N. Wilson/B. Sherrill/R. Bourke)
Al Gallico Music Corp./Algee Music Corp. BMI

"The Year that Clayton Delaney Died" – p. 44
(Tom T. Hall)
Newkeys Music Inc. BMI

"The Ballad of Forty Dollars" – p. 45
(Tom T. Hall)
Newkeys Music Inc. BMI

"The Ode to Billie Joe" – p. 45
(Bobbie Gentry)
Larry Shayne Music, Inc. ASCAP

"(I Never Promised You a) Rose Garden" – p. 48
(Joe South)
Lowery Music Co. BMI

"I Left My Heart in San Francisco" – p. 62
(D. Cross-G. Cory)
General Music Publ. Co.

"Mona Lisa" – p. 62
(Jay Livingston-Ray Evans)

"Blue Suede Shoes" – p. 68
(Carl Perkins)
Hi Lo Music, Inc. BMI

"Christmas Is Everywhere" – p. 70
(Joe Keene)
Lincoln Road Music Co. BMI

"Don't Be Cruel" – p. 96
(Blackwell-Presley)
Elvis Presley Music Inc./Travis Music Co./
Unichappell Music Corp. BMI

"All Shook Up" – p. 96
(Blackwell-Presley)
Elvis Presley Music Inc./Travis Music Co./
Unichappell Music Inc. BMI

"Great Balls of Fire" – p. 96
(Blackwell-Hammer)
Hill and Range Songs, Inc. BMI

"In the Ghetto" – p. 96
(Mac Davis)
B-N-B Music Inc./Gladys Music Inc. ASCAP

"Don't Cry Daddy" – p. 96
(Mac Davis)
Gladys Music Inc./B-N-B Music Inc. ASCAP

"Johnny B. Good" – p. 96
(Chuck Berry)
Arc Music Corp. BMI

"Sweet Little Sixteen" – p. 96
(Chuck Berry)
Arc Music Corp. BMI

"Roll Over Beethoven" – p. 96
(Chuck Berry)
Arc Music Corp. BMI

"School Days" – p. 96
(Chuck Berry)
Arc Music Corp. BMI

"Maybelline" – p. 96
(R. Frato-/A. Freed/C. Berry)
Arc Music Corp. BMI

"Memphis, Tennessee" – p. 96
(Chuck Berry)
Arc Music Corp. BMI

"Alexander's Ragtime Band" – p. 96
(Irving Berlin)

"There's No Business Like Show Business" – p.   96
(Irving Berlin)

"God Bless America" – p. 96
(Irving Berlin)

"Easter Parade" – p. 97
(Irving Berlin)

"White Christmas" – p. 97/130
(Irving Berlin)

"Jailhouse Rock" – p. 98
(Leiber-Stoller)

"Treat Me Nice" – p. 98
(Leiber-Stoller)

"Hound Dog" – p. 98
(Leiber-Stoller)
Elvis Presley Music, Inc./Lion Publishing Co. Inc.
Unichappell Music Inc. BMI

"Young Blood" – p. 98
(Leiber/Stoller/Pomus)
Tiger Music, BMI

"Searchin'" – p. 98
(Leiber-Stoller)
Tiger Music, BMI

"Charlie Brown" – p. 98
(Leiber-Stoller)
Tiger Music, BMI

"Bye Bye Love" – p. 98
(F. Bryant-B. Bryant)
Acuff-Rose Publ./House of Bryant Publ. BMI

"Wake Up Little Susie" – p. 98
(F. Bryant-B. Bryant)
Acuff-Rose Publ./House of Bryant Publ. BMI

"Rocky Top" – p. 98
(F. Bryant-B. Bryant)
House of Bryant Publ. BMI

"Rudolph The Red-Nosed Reindeer" – p. 130
(Johnny Marks)
St. Nicholas Music Corp.

Stephen Foster songs – p. 133
"Old Black Joe"
"Camptown Races"
"Jeanie with the Light Brown Hair"
"Oh! Susanna"
"Old Folks at Home"
"My Old Kentucky Home"